THE GREAT FIFA WORLD CUP ROBBERY

AND OTHER SOCCER SCANDALS

THE GREAT FIFA WORLD CUP ROBBERY

AND OTHER SOCCER SCANDALS

MIKE HOLGATE

HALSGROVE

First published in Great Britain in 2015

British Library Cataloguing-in-Publication Data
A CIP record for this title is available from the British Library

ISBN 978 0 85704 279 8

HALSGROVE
Halsgrove House,
Ryelands Business Park,
Bagley Road, Wellington, Somerset TA21 9PZ
Tel: 01823 653777   Fax: 01823 216796
email: sales@halsgrove.com

Part of the Halsgrove group of companies
Information on all Halsgrove titles is available at: www.halsgrove.com

Printed in China by the Everbest Printing Co Ltd

CONTENTS

diplomatic incident when he was charged with stealing a bracelet prior to the 1970 World Cup finals.

"Who found the cup, who found the cup, ee-aye-addio, Pickles found the cup!"

INTRODUCTION

Life is itself but a game of football
Sir Walter Scott (from *The Lifting of the Banner*, 1821)

Half a century ago in 1966, England won the World Cup for the only time in their history and the team were joined at a celebration dinner by canine hero Pickles who had found the trophy after it had been stolen from an exhibition. England and West Ham captain Bobby Moore lifted the FA Cup, European Cup Winners Cup and Jules Rimet trophy for club and country in the mid 1960s, then, found himself at the centre of a diplomatic row prior to the 1970 World Cup finals when he was framed over the theft of a bracelet from a shop in Bogota. The soccer-mad nation of Brazil were awarded the World Cup outright after winning it for the third time in 1970, then felt a sense of national disgrace when the trophy was stolen without trace in 1983.

Having previously written several books on either football club histories or true-life crimes, these unsavoury soccer incidents presented the perfect opportunity to combine the two subjects and also compile a litany of illegal activities and sleaze afflicting top domestic clubs. The stories feature murders, trophy thefts, match-fixing scandals and sleaze that have tarnished the image of the world's most popular sport. In fact, the recent exposure of Fifa as a global criminal organisation worthy of the Mafia highlights the ugly truth about the 'beautiful game':

The Beautiful Game

Trophies of silver
Cups of gold,
History stolen
Scrapped and sold.
Match-fixing scandals,
Betting rings foiled,
Cases of murder,
Footballers gaoled.
To lovers of soccer
It seems such a shame
That life can't be played
Like the beautiful game.

Mike Holgate

THE AUTHOR

Mike Holgate lives in Devon and has combined three careers as a writer, musician and librarian since obtaining a honours degree from Plymouth University in 1988. The author of several soccer and true-life crime books, he has also contributed articles to newspapers and magazines and has acted as an advisor and researcher for programmes produced by BBC Radio Devon and Granada Television.

1
THE GREAT FIFA WORLD CUP ROBBERY 2015

"We cannot allow the reputation of football and Fifa to be dragged through the mud any longer."

Sepp Blatter, President of FIFA (2015)

With England preparing to commemorate the 50th anniversary of their World Cup success in 1966, the global governing body Fifa stands accused by the US attorney-general, Loretta Lynch, of presiding over a 'World Cup of fraud', involving decades of corruption, bribery, money-laundering, racketeering and a range of organised criminal activities worthy of the Mafia.

Suspicions about the criminality at the heart of Fifa's affairs had circulated for years before the world soccer organisation was shamed in May 2015. Unbeknown to delegates, as they gathered to go through the motions of re-electing controversial Fifa president Sepp Blatter for a fifth four-year term at a convention in Zurich, Swiss and American authorities were cooperating in an hush-hush investigation. Plain-clothed police swooped in a dawn raid on seven Fifa officials in the luxury of their five star hotel and arrested them on charges of bribery and corruption. The operation was part of an FBI probe that indicted fourteen people in a precursor to the greatest sporting scandal in history.

The resulting humiliation and embarrassment suffered by Swiss national Sepp Blatter in his own country did not deter him from insisting that the presidential election should go ahead as planned. Despite a personal face-to-face plea from UEFA president and former French international Michel Platini, Blatter refused to step down and despite widespread condemnation, still won an overwhelming number of votes, with support from African and Asian delegates, to beat opposing candidate, Prince Ali Bin al-Hussein of Jordan, by a convincing margin. Defending his position to stay on by stating that the misconduct of individuals in the Fifa organisation was not his responsibility, seventy-nine year old Blatter suddenly

Sir Alf Ramsey gazes into a crystal football inscribed with the names of the 1966 World Cup team. Who could have foreseen that fifty years later the quest for the holy grail of soccer would be tarnished by scandal?

changed his mind a few days later and unexpectedly announced that he would only remain in charge until a special congress convened to elect a new leader, giving rise to speculation that his role at the centre of illegal activities was also under investigation by the FBI and US prosecutors. Gregg Dyke, the chairman of the FA, made a telling comment on the resignation: 'Clearly there's a smoking gun. It's not to do with Sepp Blatter being honourable'.

The twenty-four man Fifa executive committee is the 'cabinet' of the government of world football. Their votes decide the destination of the final stages of the World Cup. These powerful delegates are courted by kings and presidents as they tour the globe seeking the best venue (or in some cases the best deal for themselves). Bribery is reported to be rife and the American authorities are investigating alleged corruption in the bidding process to award countries the right to host the following past and future World Cup finals:

1998 France: The award was tainted by allegations that bribes were offered in the hosting process by rival bidder Morocco to Fifa vice-president Jack Warner of Trinidad and Tobago. Warner resigned in 2011 amid numerous allegations of corruption and in May 2015, a warrant was issued for his arrest by the US Department of Justice. Facing charges of fraud and racketeering, Warner reacted by threatening to release an 'avalanche' of evidence to investigators that would also implicate Fifa president Sepp Blatter.

2002 Japan: Former UEFA president Lennart Johansson of Sweden has claimed that Fifa executives were offered bribes from nations bidding to stage the finals. Following the recent scandal, Johansson urged Blatter to step down and added, 'People want us to be clean'.

2006 Germany: Rumours have been rife that the award was less than clean and allegations claim the preferred candidate supplied arms to Saudi Arabia in exchange for support for their bid. Germany beat South Africa by 12-11 votes after one member of the Fifa executive abstained. A tie would have left Sepp Blatter with the casting vote.

2010 South Africa: A *Sunday Times* undercover investigation unearthed evidence that both South Africa and Morocco had bribed officials, before Morocco had been robbed of hosting the finals after actually winning the vote. Taped conversations of these claims made by official, Ismail Bhamjee of Botswana, were subsequently handed to Sepp Blatter and Fifa in 2010. Bhamjee had resigned from the Fifa executive committee after illegally selling tickets during the previous World Cup final stages in Germany.

2014 Brazil: The FBI are reportedly investigating allegations of widespread bribes and kickbacks relating to tournament contractors and marketing deals.

2018 Russia: The host nation has denied any impropriety in the selection procedure and reacted strongly to calls to strip Russia of the event. The head of the organising committee Alexey Sorokin remarked that he was 'puzzled' by the investigation into bribe-taking and the World Cup selection process arguing that Russia had a 'good, transparent bid'. He also dismissed the wider issues commenting: 'Fifa handles billions of dollars. Naturally, there can be abuses in some places'.

2022 Qatar: Shock and disbelief greeted the news that the tiny desert state, with virtually no footballing tradition or infrastructure and a high terror risk, had won the right to host the finals. Furthermore, Fifa sanctioned moving the competition from its usual time of year in an attempt to avoid the searing summer temperatures of up to 50 degrees centigrade. An investigation by the *Sunday Times* uncovered massive corruption in the bidding process. Harmed with a cache of millions of documents provided by a whistle-blower, evidence suggested that Qatar's most senior football official Mohammed bin Hammam had allegedly 'bought' the rights with a series of 'bungs' to stage the World Cup.

England were victims of the corrupt bidding process on two occasions. In 2000, they attempted to win the nomination to host the tournament in 2006, the 40th anniversary of their World Cup win in 1966. After a campaign costing £10million, England secured five votes in the first round and only two in the second from the twenty-four strong executive of Fifa. It was generally believed at the time that hooliganism by some supporters at Euro 2000 undermined any chances of success for England. However, hope was renewed when England made a further bid to host the 2018 World Cup finals.

The procedure began in 2009 and England invested £20million competing with rival bidders and eventual winners Russia, proposed joint hosts Spain & Portugal and Belgium & Netherlands. When the decision was made in December 2010, England was surprisingly eliminated at the first hurdle after receiving just two votes. A celebrity trio of Prince William, footballer

David Beckham and Prime Minister David Cameron, who had lent their backing and good names to the project, were visibly shocked at the outcome and according to one senior FA source were 'bitterly disappointed' and 'felt lied to' having privately secured the pledges of at least five Fifa delegates – three of whom apparently reneged on their promises. A senior Fifa official, Harold Mayne-Nichols, chairman of a group tasked with assessing the competing bids, claimed that England was 'by far the strongest contender'. With England naively trying to obtain the nomination by honest means, Prince William reportedly objected to having to fawn over Fifa officials who had assembled in Zurich to decide which country should host the World Cup and was quoted as saying: 'I don't know why we have to suck up to these people'.

Criminal proceedings are likely to take years to reach resolution leaving the world governing body Fifa in crisis. If the charges are proven in a court of law, compensation will be sought by many countries that were cynically robbed of the opportunity to stage the final stages of the World Cup. When the current scandal first broke at Fifa headquarters in Switzerland, a BBC television reporter succinctly summed up the shocking situation facing world football: 'Never has the beautiful game looked so ugly'.

"They think it's all over. It is now!" The game's up for Sepp Blatter (or is it?).

"It's the F.A. Cup – I 'won' it"

2
THE GREAT
WORLD CUP HEIST
1966

Football has got to do with everything ...
the one ancient and glorious sport which
appeals to the reason and heart of England.

Arnold Bennett (*The Card*, 1911)

National football manager Alf Ramsey's confident three-year-old prediction that 'England will win the World Cup' was fulfilled on Saturday 30 July 1966. His team of 'wingless wonders' lined up in a then relatively unfamiliar 4-3-3 formation, to make full use of home advantage and defeat West Germany 4-2, with two goals scored in extra time at Wembley Stadium. Supporter Ann Smith from Manchester was awarded a cash prize by *Charles Buchan's Football Monthly* magazine when she wrote a poetic tribute to eleven newly created soccer immortals and the part they played in England's memorable golden day:

> *Oh England, our England, how great to see that win;*
> *How proudly beat a million hearts, amid the merry din,*
> *What palpitations filled the breast, what lungs felt fit to burst,*
> *When each team strove for that vital goal – thank goodness for Geoff Hurst,*
> *And captain – "Gold Cup" Bobby, defensive skill to fore;*

Nobby Stiles performs a victory dance alongside captain Bobby Moore, hat-trick hero Geoff Hurst (holding the World Cup) and England's other final scorer Martin Peters.

No wonder at the second goal supporters yelled for "Moore".
And Gordon Banks, our goalie, dependable and skilled,
His acrobatic talents and his saves just had us thrilled.

George Cohen and Ray Wilson showed ability and sense,
And played their parts tenaciously – a staunch and great defence.
Gay Nobby Stiles – who sorted out the danger shots – the grafter,
Whose Victory Dance with coveted cup, doubled us with laughter.
Great Bobby Charlton – how he played, and seized on all his chances,
But those Germans had him well marked out, spoiling his advances.
And brother Jack, at Bobby's back – he gave them all he'd got.
To Mr and Mrs Charlton – "Well done, and thanks a lot".

Young Alan Ball was everywhere, bouncing with vigour and vim,
And chasing up and down the field to help his great team win.
Geoff Hurst we will remember – how he whipped the ball into the net;
Scoring three goals, and spurring team on – how could we ever forget?
West Germany was hampered by that poacher, Roger Hunt;
Martin Peters was our hero when he put his team in front.
A really great World Final, thrilling, skilful, clean,
Fine team-work, nerve and spirit – the best World Cup Final we've seen.

Around the country there were rapturous scenes, reminiscent of Victory in Europe Day celebrating the end of the war with Germany in 1945 and the Coronation of Elizabeth II in 1953. Millions of television viewers joined with the home supporters amongst the 100 000 capacity crowd to cheer victorious captain Bobby Moore as he led his triumphant team up the steps to the royal box and received the gold Jules Rimet trophy from HM The Queen. Amidst the patriotic fervour, a recent humiliating episode was temporarily forgotten, for, earlier that year, it seemed likely that there would be nothing to present to the winners when the trophy was sensationally stolen in broad daylight from a closely guarded exhibition centre in London. For the Football Association (FA) and Sir Stanley Rous, the English president of the Federation of International Football Associations (Fifa), the situation was deeply embarrassing – three months before the World Cup finals were due to start – the host nation had failed in their duty of safekeeping and were unable to produce the trophy.

Delegates from World Cup holders Brazil, brought the one foot high gold Jules Rimet trophy weighing nine pounds to the World Cup draw in London before it was put on display at an exhibition of 'Sport with Stamps' at the Methodist Central Hall, Westminster. During a Mothering Day morning service on Sunday 20 March, a thief entered the building and mingled with the congregation before forcing open a rear door to the exhibition room then, ignoring stamp collections valued at £3million calmly stole the football trophy by removing a small padlock at the back of the glass-fronted cabinet. Incredibly, four security guards were on duty tasked with keeping a constant eye on the historic trophy, but at the crucial moment, all of them had been otherwise engaged, patrolling the lower ground floor of the exhibition, enjoying a tea break or answering the call of nature. A police investigation established that the theft had happened after 11am and was not discovered until midday. During the time when the exhibition was open, two guards had been stationed either side of the glass case containing the World Cup, but in his company's defence, the head of the security firm responsible for the exhibition offered a lame excuse to the press: 'The pressure of security was not considered quite so serious when the hall was closed to the public'. He also described the adverse reaction from all around the world as 'very terrible and embarrassing', adding that the crime had placed him under a 'great strain' although he believed the hail of criticism that had been received to be 'harsh and a little unjust'. The governing body, recognising the enormity of the damage done to their reputation, issued an apologetic statement: 'The FA deeply regrets this most unfortunate incident, which inevitably brings discredit to both the FA and this country'.

A suspicious-looking 'thin' individual wearing a 'dark coat' had been seen loitering in the hall by some people attending the church service and a number of telephone calls were made to newspapers and news agencies attributing the theft to a student rag stunt. As a result, police questioned a scholar at the West Ham College of Technology but were eventually satisfied that he had no connection with the crime. Then, two days after the daring raid, Chelsea and Football Association chairman Joe Mears received a telephone call from someone calling himself 'Jackson' who told him: 'There will be a parcel at Stamford Bridge tomorrow. Follow the instructions inside'. As promised, on the Wednesday after the theft the parcel arrived containing part of the lining from the Jules Rimet trophy and a ransom letter demanding £15 000 in five and one pound notes with a warning about the consequences of not responding or contacting the police: 'No doubt you view with very much concern the loss of the World Cup. To me it is only so much scrap gold. If I don't hear from you by Thursday or Friday at the latest I assume it's one for the POT'. During a follow-up call, 'Jackson' made the following promise: 'Give me the £15 000 on Friday and the cup will be delivered by cab on Saturday'. As instructed by the criminal contact, Mears placed a message in Thursday's edition of the *London Evening News*: 'Willing to do business, Joe', but sensibly informed the police of his involvement. On Friday, Detective Inspector Len Buggy of the Flying Squad called at the home of Joe Mears to brief him about the intended rendezvous with the thief, but the stressed-out FA chairman was bedridden with angina. D.I. Buggy arranged for Mrs Mears to speak to 'Jackson' when he telephoned and explain that as her husband was ill, his assistant 'McPhee' would deliver the ransom. The revised agreement was made and Buggy, posing as 'McPhee', drove Joe Mears' car to meet 'Jackson' at Battersea Park. The policeman was carrying only £500 in bundles of notes mixed with sheets of newspaper to try and fool the thief, but the operation went badly wrong when the suspicious crook spotted a police backup van following the car and fled from the scene. The police gave chase and arrested 'Jackson' who was quickly identified as Edward Betchley. When questioned it transpired that the prisoner did not have the trophy and he insisted that he had not been part of the heist but had merely agreed to accept £500 of the ransom money to act as a 'go-between' for a man he knew only as 'The Pole'. The police realised that they had hardly apprehended 'Mr Big', for Betchley, a forty-six year old market stall holder, had only one previous conviction for receiving tins of stolen corned beef in 1954. Scotland Yard's informants in the criminal underworld were unable to identify the suspect referred to by Betchley as 'The Pole' and no one else was ever arrested for the crime.

With the whereabouts of the Jules Rimet trophy still a mystery, the FA took steps to produce a replica for the final. However, when the original trophy had been missing for a week, the nation was finally spared further humiliation by a black-and-white mongrel called Pickles. While being taken for an evening walk by his owner, David Corbett, the dog wandered away from their home in the leafy suburb of Upper Norwood, London, and became absorbed with digging near a hedge. When Mr Corbett came to drag his pet away, he discovered that Pickles had unearthed a parcel wrapped in newspaper. Tearing it open and seeing the familiar gold symbolic winged figure inside, Corbett excitedly ran into his flat and shouted to his wife, 'I've found the World Cup! I've found the World Cup!' Still wearing his slippers, Corbett immediately rushed with his find to Gypsy Hill police station in Crystal Palace and from there was taken for quizzing to Scotland Yard. During the interview his story was treated with suspicion and he faced a barrage of questions until the early hours of the morning before his alibi was accepted and he was released just four hours before starting his shift as a Thames lighterman at 6.30am. According to research carried out for a television documentary, 'Who Stole the Cup?' broadcast by Channel Four in 2006, Edward Betchley made a deal with the police whilst being held on remand in Brixton Prison. He intimated that if a certain lady friend was allowed to visit him in jail, and she was not followed by the police when she left, then the cup's location would be

Pickles was the toast of Fleet Street.

subsequently revealed. The prisoner got his wish and two days later Pickles received the glory for finding the trophy.

Suddenly thrust into the media spotlight, Pickles' fame briefly matched that of canine film stars Lassie and Rin Tin Tin as he became a national hero and the toast of Fleet Street. When the England team celebrated their cup final victory with a banquet, Pickles was invited along and arrived at the hotel just in time to lick the players' plates clean. During the tournament, members of the England team earned a £60 match fee with reserves receiving £30 for each of the six games played during the competition, and the FA also paid a bonus of £1000 to each of the twenty-two man squad for winning the World Cup. However, the real winner was David Corbett, the owner of Pickles, who received almost £6000 (the modern-day equivalent of over £180 000) for recovering the missing trophy. The lucky recipient revealed to the press that he was 'amazed' to discover that Joe Mears had put in a competing claim to the loss adjusters. The Chairman of the Football Association defended his decision explaining that he felt entitled to the money as a consequence of all the 'work and worry' he had endured during the negotiations with the 'go-between' Edward Betchley: 'As a result I told the police. My home became a headquarters and several times the man telephoned me giving me various instructions during the following days. He has now been arrested and that is the basis of my claim'. Joe Mears' stance in expecting an ex-gratia payment, for recovering the trophy that his organisation was responsible for losing, was greeted with derision by sections of the press. The ill-judged claim was swiftly withdrawn and his wife disclosed that her husband believed the matter should have been kept secret: 'He is very upset about all this publicity. I do not think that the assessors should have told Mr Corbett my husband's name'.

By a strange quirk of fate, in what may be termed the 'curse of the cup', the three principles in this saga, Joe Mears, Edward Betchley and Pickles were to meet with tragically premature deaths:

Manager Alf Ramsey, the team that won the final and Jimmy Greaves who played in the first three matches of the tournament before injury ruled him out.

Joe Mears was robbed of the opportunity to see England win the World Cup when the health problems, experienced through the stress of dealing with the theft of the cup, returned to claim his life. The sixty-one year old suffered a fatal heart attack during a business trip to Oslo on the 1st July – just ten days before England played the opening match of the tournament.

Edward Betchley admitted charges of 'being concerned with larceny after the fact' and 'demanding money with menaces' at a hastily arranged trial at the Central Criminal Court on 9 July. He was sentenced to two years imprisonment by the judge, Mr Justice Lyell, who rejected the defendant's claim that he had been tempted to become involved by the offer of £500 as he was in financial difficulties: 'I think you were hoping to get a very much larger share of the £15 000. No other supposition makes sense'. In 1969, a year after his release from prison, Betchley died from emphysema aged only forty-nine.

Pickles' owner, David Corbett reportedly pocketed cheques donated by the loss adjusters (£3000), The National Sporting Club (£1000) Fulham chairman and showbiz personality Tommy Trinder (£1000), the Gillette Razor company (£500), and from a London osteopath, who had treated injured England footballers, Walter Max (£150). In addition, Pickles' inquisitive sniffing brought a 'Dog of the Year' award from the National Canine Defence League, a free year's supply of doggie treats and television appearances on children's programmes *Magpie* and *Blue Peter*. However, in 1971, Pickles' time in the celebrity spotlight came to an untimely end when he rashly reverted to type by chasing a cat. Pulling away from David Corbett's six-year-old son who was taking him for a walk, the dog escaped and disappeared into some gardens. After searching for over an hour, the distraught owner found Pickles' body hanging from a tree. The dog's choke chain had become entangled in a branch as he raced after his feline quarry. Fittingly, the canine hero was buried in the garden of the house that had been purchased with the money awarded for recovering the World Cup.

At the height of his fame, Pickles starred as himself alongside Lawrence Harvey, Lionel Jeffries, Eric Sykes and June Whitfield in the movie spoof *The Spy with the Cold Nose* (1966) and it could be said that the FA's handling of the stolen cup affair was a comedy of errors worthy of the plot of a classic film produced by Ealing Studios. A film theme was acknowledged in the FA's official review of the World Cup final of 1966. The authors, recalling a game featuring a West German equaliser in the last minute of normal time, a hotly disputed England goal to take the lead and a famous victory sealed with the last kick of a thirty-two match tournament, summed up the remarkable sporting occasion, 'No more gripping finale could have been offered as a product of the scriptwriter's art. If it had been fiction instead of fact, it would have been regarded incredulously'. Indeed, no scriptwriter could have topped BBC television commentator Kenneth

Wolstenholme's brilliant improvisation when a handful of supporters invaded the pitch just as Geoff Hurst latched on to a long ball from Bobby Moore and burst through the opposition defence to complete the first ever hat-trick in a world cup final: 'Some people are on the pitch! They think it's all over! … Then, as the ball flew into the top corner of the net … 'It is now!

"They think it's all over! … It is now!"

3
THE FA CUP BURGLARY
1895

The Cup belongs as much to the Davids as to the Goliaths. They are all part of the same mosaic which sprang from the original 'little tin idol'.

Geoffrey Green, football correspondent of *The Times* (1972)

The 1895 FA Cup final was the first to be played at the Crystal Palace and scores of special trains carried rival fans from the Midlands to London to watch an eagerly anticipated match between Aston Villa and West Bromwich Albion. To add spice to the occasion, this was the third cup final meeting between the two clubs in eight years. The 'Villains' emerged as 2-0 victors in the 1887 FA Cup final, but the 'Throstles' avenged this defeat with a shock 3-0 win for the underdogs in 1892. However, on 28 April 1895, before a crowd of 42 500, the destiny of the FA Cup in the third final between the clubs was surprisingly decided within a minute of the start. Having won the toss Albion chose to play with the sun at their backs and a stiff breeze blowing in their favour. Aston Villa kicked off the match and forty seconds later fired in what was to be the only goal of the game. Goal hero Bob Chatt was to hold the record for the fastest FA Cup final goal until Louis Saha gave Everton a dream start by scoring in twenty-five seconds before his side lost 1-2 to Chelsea in 2009.

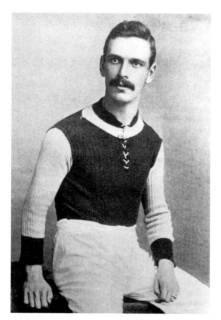

John Devey was the last captain to lift the original 'little tin idol'.

Aston Villa skipper John Devey was presented with the FA Cup in 1895 and the *Sunday Times* duly reported: 'At length the much-talked about game is over and the Football Association Challenge Cup will during the ensuing twelve months remain in the possession of the far-famed Aston Villa'. Embarrassingly for the 'Villains', this was not to be the case, as five months later the cup affectionately known as the 'little tin idol' went missing, stimulating a sensational banner headline in *The Weekly Standard* which pronounced 'A Football Catastrophe - The English Cup Stolen'.

Aston Villa with the FA Cup in 1895.

Late in August 1895, Aston Villa allowed the FA Cup to be exhibited in the shop window of a local boot manufacturer and sports outfitters owned by William Shillcock, a prominent club member and business friend of Villa chairman William McGregor – the renowned 'Father of the Football League'. Within a fortnight of the cup going on display, thieves climbed a high wall on to a flat projection on the roof of the shop adjoining the workshop and, tearing off the zinc covering, made a hole eighteen inches by twelve in the ceiling of the shop. Letting themselves down they then took the cup. The perpetrators ransacked the cash till which contained only two shillings (10p) but did not touch the valuable stock. The *Birmingham Daily Post* reported how Mr Shillcock, who did not live on the premises, unlocked his shop in Newtown Row early on Wednesday 11 September and was shocked to discover the scene of an 'appalling sacrilege':

He walked into a room behind the shop, and on returning saw the cash drawer on the counter. Then his suspicions were aroused, and on looking round he saw the floor at one side covered with plaster, and on looking above there was a hole through the roof. The shop is a building of one storey, which has been added to what was originally the front of a private house. By its side is an entry, somewhat narrow, and as the hole in the roof is on the side adjoining the entry the only suggestion is that the robber or robbers got on to the roof from the entry, and that this was done by climbing with a hand and foot on each wall. Some of the footmarks on the roof are those of persons wearing india rubber-soled boots, so that the climb would not be so difficult to a muscular person wearing such shoes. The lead on the roof was stripped off, and the lath and plaster broken through. To get back again a pair of steps found in the shop were used. Beyond the theft of the cup and some few shillings taken from the cash-drawer, nothing else has been missed from the premises. Under these circumstances the object of the robbery seems somewhat obscure as, apart from the historic value of the cup, the silver, when melted down, would be worth not more than £5 in the present state of the silver market.

Football Association rules dictated that the Cup-holders had to guarantee the safe-keeping of the trophy and the winning club was bound by the following clause:

We members and representatives of the club, having been declared to have won the Football Association Challenge Cup, and the same having been delivered to us by the said Association, do hereby, on behalf of the said club, individually and collectively engage to return the same to the secretary of the Association for the time being, on or before the 1st day of March next, in good order and condition, and in accordance with the rules. And provided such Cup is destroyed or damaged by fire or any other cause, or lost while under our care, we agree to refund the Association the amount of the original value, or cost of thorough repair.

Aston Villa were fined £25 by the FA for the loss of the cup and, under the terms of the above agreement, were obliged to pay a sum of £200 to replace the trophy. William Shillcock had given a similar undertaking to reimburse the club for the same amount. Despite a reward of £10 for information offered by the shop owner, the 'little tin idol' was never recovered and a distraught William Shillcock later revealed his shame over the affair, 'I pictured myself a ruined man, a hated individual'. A satirical editorial in the *Birmingham Daily Mail* scornfully urged the culprit to come forward and accept the acclaim due to him for the historic crime:

It takes some of the our best football teams years to win the English Cup; some never win it at all; yet it only took Bill Sikes a few minutes with his clever forward play to capture the Cup, and put it in his own pocket. He does not seem to have been in front of goal more than a quarter of an hour. Whoever he is, William has made his mark. It will be a pity for various reasons if his identity remains a mystery. It will rob history of a great name. Christopher Columbus, Napoleon Bonaparte, Admiral Drake, Tom Sayers, Shakespeare and Wellington have each a niche in the Temple of Fame, but there should just be a corner reserved for the man who burgled the English Cup. Even if he should get six months for it, he will be very foolish if he does not come forward and claim the immortality that awaits him. He ought to rise to a proper sense of the importance of his work. If he consigns the precious Cup to the melting pot and preserves an inglorious anonymity, he will prove himself a mean, miserable, soulless person. And he must remember this; that a man who has burgled the English Cup cannot descend into ordinary crime. If he continues in business he must live up to his best work. It is hard to see how

£10 REWARD.

STOLEN!

From the Shop Window of W. Shillcock, Football Outfitter, Newtown Row, Birmingham, between the hour of 9-30 p.m. on Wednesday, the 11th September, and 7-30 a.m., on Thursday, the 12th inst., the

ENGLISH CUP,

the property of Aston Villa F.C. The premises were broken into between the hours named, and the Cup, together with cash in drawer, stolen.

The above Reward will be paid for the recovery of the Cup, or for information as may lead to the conviction of the thieves.

Information to be given to the Chief of Police, or to Mr. W. Shillcock, 73, Newtown Row.

The offer of a reward failed to recover the stolen cup.

he can improve upon last night's work, unless he makes up his mind to have a try for the Holy Coat of Treves, Cleopatra's Needle or the Dome of St Paul's. It will thus be seen that he has placed himself in a rather awkward position. He had better rest contented with and take credit for his one great achievement, and in the seclusion of Winson Green he might occupy his time on a standard work for the sporting papers, entitled "How I Won the English Cup in Ten Minutes".

In the immediate aftermath of the crime, no Dickensian 'Bill Sikes' character accepted the local newspaper's challenge to turn himself into the authorities and the *Birmingham Daily Mail* commented further:

The footballers of England will be in a fever until this tremendous mystery is solved. It is awful to think of the possibilities. For aught anyone knows to the contrary, the vile vandal who purloined the Cup may be drinking his dinner beer out of it at the present moment in the burglar's humble but happy home. He cannot offer such a well-known article for sale by auction. The poor little Cup may by this time have been consigned to the melting pot. This is too terrible to think of. If the miscreant has done this, heaven help him if he falls into the hands of the police. No English gaol will be strong enough to protect him from the rough justice of Judge Lynch.

The original FA Cup, which had been contested for since 1872, was replaced by a replica supplied by former Aston Villa and England international Howard Vaughton who, following his retirement from football, had joined the family business of silversmith's in Birmingham. The 'new' trophy was produced from a cast taken by another Midland club Wolverhampton Wanders following their FA Cup final win over Everton in 1893. The Vaughton version would continue to be competed for until it was presented to Lord Kinnard to commemorate his twenty-one years as FA President in 1910.

The mystery of the unsolved case of the missing FA Cup remained a 'whodunnit' worthy of the pen of contemporary writer, and former Portsmouth goalkeeper, Sir Arthur Conan Doyle, who might have given a whole new meaning to the phrase, 'The game's afoot Watson' by allowing his fictional creation Sherlock Holmes to investigate 'The Affair of the Little Tin Idol'. It was decades later before suspects eventually emerged after an octogenarian habitual criminal sold his story to the *Sunday Pictorial*. The tabloid published a front-page exclusive on 23 February 1958 with the headline: 'Sensational Confession Ends Soccer's Biggest Riddle'. The source of the newspaper article was Harry Burge who had spent half his life in prison and emerged from a welfare hostel, where he had been placed after receiving a sentence of seven years' preventative detention for stealing from cars, to stake a belated claim to fame. He described how the silver cup had been melted down on the night it was stolen and made into fake half-crown coins [12p]. However, his poverty-stricken lifestyle cast doubt on his motives. There were discrepancies in his story and the belief grew that he may have simply approached the press to obtain a much-needed pay out. Burge was photographed re-enacting how he entered the rear door of the shop by using a small crowbar and also admitted stealing several pairs of football boots during the raid. This account contradicted contemporary news reports establishing that the thief had entered and left the premises via the hole in the roof and that no goods had been taken. Whatever the truth about the involvement of Harry Burge, the police showed no interest in his belated 'confession' by pursuing the matter through the courts. However, historic CID records reveal details of forging gangs operating in the Newtown area where thieves had been arrested for stealing silver and making counterfeit half-crowns that were passed off through betting at the old Birmingham racecourse at Bromford Bridge. Burge was a housebreaker and opportunistic thief but had never been accused of forgery while amassing an appalling criminal record of nearly fifty convictions in a sixty-year career stretching back to 1897. The old rogue passed away in 1964 and the next suspect was unmasked when the *Birmingham Mail* carried a story in 1975. This time the finger of suspicion was pointed at the late Joseph Piecewright, a felon who had served imprisonment for counterfeiting coins. The informant was his grandson, Edwin Tranter from Acocks Green. The renewed interest in the case stimulated an investigation carried out by the team that produced the Aston Villa fan magazine *Claret and Blue*. As a result, their findings revealed that four men may have been involved in the theft. According to this theory, when the historic cup was stolen it was immediately melted down and taken to a receiver who told them that the metal was an alloy, not pure silver, and offered the derisory sum of 'Ten bob [50p]. Take it or leave'. Actual names of suspects did not materialise until BBC Radio WM broadcast a follow-up programme about the historic theft. Listening to the programme was eighty-year-old widow Violet Stait who recalled that her late husband Jack had told her before they were married that, 'Our dad pinched that Cup out of Shillcock's window' and when the courting couple were walking by a row of back-to-back houses near the bootmaker's shop

Suspect John 'Stosher' Tait

he added, 'This is the yard where our dad helped to melt the Cup down'. Amongst his transgressions, Violet's moustachioed father-in-law, John 'Stosher' Stait, was gaoled for two months in January 1891 for stealing brass from his employers – a local firm of metal rollers. Charged with Stait was marine store dealer Thomas Barret who was fined £5 for receiving the stolen metal. The *Claret and Blue* team led by editor Bernard Gallagher took this new lead seriously and spent months on their inquiry verifying facts before coming to the conclusion that in all probability, 'Stosher' Stait, was one of the crooks, although, the jury is still out on the involvement of his possible accomplices Harry Burge, Joseph Piecewright, Thomas Barret, or the ultimate fate of the first incarnation of soccer's first great 'little tin idol' – the FA Cup. Aston Villa wasted little time in lifting the replacement trophy in 1897. In a momentous season the club emulated Preston North End by becoming only the second club to achieve the magical League and Cup Double. Following their exciting 3-2 FA Cup final win over Everton, a correspondent of *The Penny Illustrated* recalled the club's unfortunate experience with the old trophy and commented with classic understatement: 'It is morally certain I think that Aston Villa will not risk letting the cup won on Saturday go out of their custody'.

3
THE THEFT OF THE EUROPEAN CUP
1982

*We've had two cups stolen, that's
more than the Blues have won!*

Online Aston Villa fan taunts rivals Birmingham City

If Oscar Wilde had been a football supporter, he may have been excused for thinking, 'To lose one cup may be regarded as misfortune, to lose both looks like carelessness'. Yet, amazingly, this is the bizarre fate that befell Aston Villa with the theft of the FA Cup in 1895 and the temporary loss of the European Cup in 1982. In the immediate aftermath of the first 'misfortune', the *Birmingham Daily Mail* described how: 'A mighty infamy rests upon Birmingham… Today the whole football world stands aghast at this appalling sacrilege… The impious hands that coveted the Holy Grail supplied quite a commonplace felony compared with the theft of the English Cup. Colonel Blood's attempt upon the Crown Jewels was simply a vulgar piece of housebreaking by the side of the majestic bit of crib-cracking last night... And what will become of Aston Villa? The penalty for losing the Cup is something lingering with boiling oil in it'.

The 'Villains' splendid playing record quickly helped them to live down any embarrassment suffered over the FA Cup affair. They have become the fifth most decorated club in English football history by winning nineteen major domestic competitions with five League Cup final victories, seven cup final wins and seven Football League Championships. However, Aston Villa's greatest honour was achieved when the club surprised the soccer world by winning the European Cup in 1982.

Aston Villa made a late bid for the Football League Championship (now the Premier League) in the 1980-81 campaign, coming from behind to deservedly take the title for the first time in seventy years. After playing forty-two games with two points for a win and one for a draw, they amassed sixty points, four ahead of runners-up Ipswich. Recent League Championship and European Cup winners, Liverpool and Nottingham Forest were both left trailing in Villa's wake as the Midlands club dramatically improved on the previous season when they had finished only seventh. Manager Ron Saunders had taken charge of the club in 1974 and transformed a struggling club into League Cup winners and runners-up in the Second Division in his first campaign. Promoted to the top tier, the team steadily made progress before topping the Football League. Saunders was a strict disciplinarian who utilised a tough training regime. Amazingly, in their Championship season, Villa used only fourteen players all season and seven of the players were ever-presents. Saunders would obviously have had no time for the modern-day squad rotation system, probably believing that players would get enough rest when they retired. Although the manager had a dour image and a reputation for playing unimaginative football that did not always endear him to the public, he built an attractive side at Villa Park captained by Dennis Mortimer, who formed an impressive midfield axis with Gordon Cowan and Des Bremner, while there was flair in abundance up front with winger Tony Morley supplying a potent strike force of Peter Withe and Gary Shaw. More honours were to be achieved by Aston Villa without Ron Saunders who quit over a contractual dispute and departed in February 1982 to take up an appointment with neighbours and fierce rivals Birmingham City – whom he promptly saved from the imminent threat of relegation. At this stage of the season, Aston Villa had slipped to nineteenth in the league but had reached the quarter-finals of the European Cup. Suddenly, first-team coach Tony Barton was thrust into the hot seat to replace Saunders and, having already seen off Valur Reykjavik (Iceland) and Dynamo Berlin (East Germany) the manager successfully steered the club past Dynamo Kiev (Russia) and Anderlecht (Belgium), to reach the final played against the formidable German team, Bayern Munich, at Feyenoord Stadium in Rotterdam on 26 May 1982. Former winners of the trophy, Bayern Munich were firm favourites with the bookmakers and within ten minutes of the start, Villa suffered a severe setback when goalkeeper Jimmy Rimmer, who had been fighting a losing battle with a neck injury, signalled to the bench that he was unable to continue and sadly walked off the field. He was replaced by substitute Nigel Spinks, making only his second first team appearance in three years, who proceeded to give a heroic display, preserving a clean sheet and making a string of stunning saves. The team emerged triumphant thanks to a mishit shot in the 67th minute by Peter

The goal that won the European Cup for Villa: "Oh, it must be and it is. It's Peter Withe!"

Withe who converted a Tony Morley cross which bobbled off his shin and went in off the inside of the goalpost to ensure a 1-0 victory. ITV sportscaster Brian Moore's commentary for the move leading up to that winner was immortalised on a banner displayed in the North Stand at Villa Park. It read, 'Shaw, Williams, prepared to venture down the left. There's a good ball in for Tony Morley. Oh, it must be and it is. It's Peter Withe!'

Aston Villa's success continued a period of dominance for Football League clubs in bringing the European Cup back to England for the sixth year in a row. However, having performed brilliantly to win the trophy, they were to lose it in haphazard style when two players, Colin Gibson and Gordon Cowans, placed the most prized silverware in Europe in the boot of a car and drove off for a get-together with supporters at the Fox Inn at Hopwas near Tamworth. What happened next was to remain a closely guarded secret for twenty-eight years and details surrounding the incredible story only came to light when photographs of cops holding the trophy were found in a police station drawer and became public for the first time in May 2010. When interviewed, former fullback Colin Gibson recalled, how, in celebratory mood, the pair carried the gigantic European Cup weighing 15kg into the pub to 'show it to the fans and let them have their pictures taken with it'. After enjoying a few drinks and taking part in a competitive darts match the players were horrified when someone shouted out, 'The cup's gone, it's been stolen'. A few hours later, the mystery of the missing cup was solved a hundred miles away in Sheffield when a man calling

Gordon Cowans was playing darts when the trophy was stolen.

himself 'Eric Sykes', the name of the popular comedy actor who had once starred in a film alongside canine World Cup hero Pickles, walked into West Bar police station. Mick Greenough, the officer on duty that night recalled: 'I remember the lad on the desk walked through to the control room and said, "We've got a man at the front desk who says he's got the European Cup in the car". So off he trotted and next thing the swing doors go and there he is at the front desk with the European Cup, with claret and blue ribbons on'. Graham Wragg, then a police constable, rang the West Midland police to try and find out where the cup had come from but before he could say anything he was cut off after being told that they were busy investigating a 'major incident'. 'So we rang back and said, "We think we know what your major incident is … We think we've got the European Cup here, would that be connected to it?" There was a bit of a silence and they said "We're coming to fetch it"'. While the night shift at West Bar were waiting for the trophy to be collected by the West Midland force, the young men, who had recently formed a soccer team, took this once-in-a-lifetime opportunity to form two sides and hold their own competition by staging an impromptu indoor game with the feted European Cup at stake. Using a scene of crime camera, a photograph was taken for posterity with uniformed officers posing with the prized trophy.

Tantalisingly, the real identity of the man who turned in the trophy to the police station was not disclosed. However, following the news revealing the background behind the story, Roger Grey came forward and related that a former flatmate, twenty-eight year old Adrian Reed was responsible for the disappearance of the trophy. 'My recollection is Adrian turned up late one night and came in holding the European Cup.' The friends had a few drinks and at one point the heavy cup was accidentally dropped down the stairs and suffered a 'few dints and a twisted handle'. He believed that Adrian Reed had 'spontaneously borrowed' the Cup to show off and meant no harm: 'He was a loveable rogue, he would do anything for his friends, a really nice bloke. He was so charming he could talk the hind legs off a donkey'. Adrian was persuaded by his friend to turn himself into the police who fortunately saw the humour of the situation and as a consequence, no charges were brought against the culprit. Graham Wragg lost touch with his friend in the 1980s and later heard the sad news that his old flatmate had been killed in a car crash.

Manager Tony Barton and the Villa squad with the European Cup.

Landlord of the Fox Inn at the time of the cup's disappearance was John Bayliss. He was an ardent Birmingham City fan and a future chairman of Tamworth FC but had journeyed to Rotterdam to support Aston Villa in the European Cup final as his pub was a popular haunt of the Villa players. He confirmed the story told by Graham Wragg: 'I remember that the cup was going around the customers and a lot of them were having their photographs taken. Then, one guy, Adrian Reed, took it and said he just wanted a picture outside with his car. He never came back so we called the police. They stayed with us and we didn't hear anything until about 3am, which is when we got the call from police in Sheffield. I didn't know Adrian that well, but he lived locally. We obviously banned him after that, but I had never had any problem with him before'.

With the European Cup safely recovered and consigned to the club trophy cabinet, Aston Villa then focused their sights on the European Super Cup contested between themselves as holders of the European Cup and the winners of the European Cup Winners, Barcelona, played over two legs in January 1983. The first encounter away in Spain resulted in a single goal defeat at the Camp Nou stadium. Aston Villa boss Tony Barton was less than impressed with the performance of his team, conceding, 'We were very lucky to get away with a 1-0 defeat'. However, he was more than pleased with the result and the deficit was overcome in an ill-tempered return at Villa Park when

Aston Villa captain Dennis Mortimer lifts the European Cup.

Gary Shaw levelled the overall score after a nail-biting 80 minutes. The match went into extra time and the 'Villains' ran out winners with a further two goals – a 100th minute penalty converted by Gordon Cowans followed up four minutes later with a goal from Ken McNaught. The score on the night was 3-0 and the overall final score a convincing 3-1 victory over the Spanish giants.

Disappointingly, the European Super Cup final failed to provide a glittering showpiece worthy of a major final. Furthermore, it was an occasion that shamed football when seven Barcelona players were booked and two sent off. A correspondent surveyed the battlefield for the *Times*:

It was a night, sadly, of utter disgrace. The two Kings of Europe met at Villa Park for supposedly a regal occasion to decide the rightful ownership to the continental throne. Instead the two hours were filled with football of stunning mediocrity and the most ugly brutality surely to be witnessed in this country. Aston Villa won the European Super Cup in the end but that hardly matters. What does matter is that this honourable game was torn to unacceptable shreds, reduced to a ragged farce by the sheer cynicism of Barcelona.

Striker Peter Withe walked off with his shirt soaked in blood flowing from a facial wound, just one of several home players who were the victims of savage assaults. In the hostile atmosphere, Villa footballers did not escape admonishment as Gibson and McNaught received yellow cards and defender Alan Evans was dismissed late in extra time for a second bookable offence in the game that went down in history as 'The Bloody Battle of Villa Park'. So ended a remarkable period in Aston Villa's chequered history when a team with a novice manager and a novice goalkeeper improbably proved that inexperience can win the day and they remain only the fourth English team alongside Manchester United, Liverpool and Nottingham Forest to land the European Cup – a feat that was commemorated by fan Doug O'Brien who attended the final and wrote about the experience in the following song:

Rotterdam 82

We're all going to Rotterdam
Each and every Villa fan,
Shout Villa, Aston Villa
Cause we're the pride of all England;
We're the greatest in the land
We're Villa, Aston Villa
Aston Villa are the greatest football team.

Withey scores in Rotterdam
He runs to all the Villa fans,
Shout Villa, Aston Villa.
And Denis Mortimer lifts the cup,
Triumphant Villa fans erupt;
Oh Villa, Aston Villa
Aston Villa are the greatest football team.

We've all been to Rotterdam
We're European Champions,
We're Villa, Aston Villa
Cause we're the greatest football team,
Villa the best you've ever seen.
We're Villa, Aston Villa,
Aston Villa are the greatest football team.

C'mon you lions, c'mon you lions,
Yes Aston Villa are the greatest football team.

4
THE ILLEGAL
PAYMENT SCANDAL
1906

In a sense the Stanley Matthews,
Tom Finney and George Best of his day,
Billy Meredith had a career as eventful
off the field as on it [and] proved a
frequent trial to officialdom.

Geoffrey Green, football correspondent of *The Times* (1985)

Manchester City won their first major trophy when they defeated Bolton Wanderers 1-0 in the first all Lancashire FA Cup final in 1904. City skipper Billy Meredith was the man of the match and earned this tribute from the *Manchester Evening Chronicle*: 'It was indeed appropriate that City's captain should score the goal which brought the cup to Manchester. He is the oldest playing member of the club, its most brilliant exponent, and, without doubt, the best outside-right in the kingdom'. Two days after the cup final, Manchester City lost their final league match of the season away at Everton which ended their hopes of accomplishing the 'double' as they finished runners-up in the championship to Sheffield Wednesday.

On the eve of the FA Cup final, Billy Meredith had been voted the Football League's most popular player, ahead of Steve Bloomer (Derby County)

44

An artist's impression of Billy Meredith's winning goal in the 1904 FA Cup final.

and Bob Crompton (Blackburn Rovers), in a poll conducted amongst the readers of sports journal the *Umpire*. Dubbed 'The Welsh Wizard' and 'The Lloyd George of Soccer', Billy Meredith moved from Welsh league side Chirsk and spent ten years with Manchester City before leading them to success in the FA Cup and their highest position in the First Division. However, the fortunes of Manchester City would suffer a dramatic reversal when they became embroiled in scandal the following season. The cup holders were eliminated at an early stage, but once again made a strong challenge for the league championship. With one game to play, City were level on points with Newcastle United at the top of the table, before slipping into third place after losing the last game of the season 2-3 away against Aston Villa. In an ill-tempered game, City striker Sandy Turnbull and Villa defender, Alex Leake, escaped censure from the referee when they traded punches in an off-the-ball incident. Fighting continued in the dressing rooms after the match and, following an investigation, Sandy Turnbull was suspended for a month. Worse was to follow when an unnamed 'gentleman' from 'Birmingham' reported 'a most interesting conversation' he had overheard before the game and alleged that Billy Meredith had offered opposing captain Alex Leake £10 to throw the game. During a subsequent inquiry, Leake, reluctantly admitted that the comment had been made, although he had simply 'laughed it off' as a joke. Meredith denied the charges of attempted bribery but was found culpable and in August 1905, received a season-long suspension from the Football Association. Banned from playing until April 1906 and also deprived of wages and a benefit match in honour of his ten years' service with the club, team manager Tom Maley wrote a letter assuring the player that he would be subsidised for his trouble: 'My Dear Billy, The unexpected has, I am sorry to say, happened and we are to be denied the pleasure of giving to you a well-deserved benefit... We have determined to see that all that is reasonable and just in this matter is done on your behalf... I don't think... that you will be the loser'.

Meredith became increasingly upset when he failed to receive an under the counter financial settlement from Manchester City and decided to 'blow the whistle' on a system of illegal payments that had been made to players in contravention of the maximum wage structure governed by the rules of the Football League. The aftermath of this latest scandal was to have a devastating effect on the club. The aggrieved player, finally admitting his guilt over the bribery affair which, he claimed, was with the knowledge of the manager and rest of the team, wrote an open letter containing damning allegations that was published in the *Athletic News*:

The club put aside the rule that no player should receive more than £4 a week. From 1902 I had been paid £6 a week... The season we carried off the Cup, I also received £53 in bonuses for games won and drawn... Altogether, the club paid in bonuses £654.12s 6d. The team delivered the goods and the club paid for the goods delivered and both sides were satisfied.

An FA Commission convened in London on 31 May 1906. It was presided over by long-serving chairman Charles Clegg known as the 'Napoleon of Football'. A former England international before becoming an eminent soccer administrator, Clegg was a product of amateur 'gentlemen' footballers and had vehemently opposed professionalism – predicting that it would have a corrupting influence on the game. A deeply religious person who frowned on drinking and gambling, Charles Clegg's favourite saying was 'nobody gets lost on a straight road', therefore, he was horrified to learn an investigation into Manchester City's affairs had established that home match attendances had been falsified, with a portion of the gate receipts put into a secret bank account from which illegal payments were made to the team. Players and officials had been questioned and admitted being party to many irregularities in wage payments which exceeded the legal maximum of £208 a year (now equivalent to £20,000). Manchester City were dealt with severely, receiving a fine of £250, while the club chairman, Waltham Forrest, who had already resigned, was banned for life from acting in any capacity involved with football under the jurisdiction of the Football Association. A similar punishment, although later lifted, was imposed on manager, Tom Maley. All five directors of the club were ordered to resign and seventeen players were suspended from taking part in football until New Year's Day 1907. In addition, the players were fined the following amounts: £100 Billy Meredith and midfielder George Livingstone; £75 centre-half Tommy Hynds and fullback Johnny McMahon; £50 goalkeeper Jack Hillman, striker Sandy Turnbull, winger Frank Booth, fullback Herbert Burgess, halfback Sammy Frost, forward Jimmy Bannister, centre-forward Billy Gillespie, defender Billy Holmes and halfback R. Dearden; £25 goalkeeper John Edmondson, fullback R Davidson, utility player WJ Lyon, halfback Sam Ashworth (the latter, deemed to be an amateur at the time of the offences, was henceforth declared a professional). The fines paid by club and players, totalling £1,150 (the modern equivalent of £100,000), were donated to Manchester charities after deduction of expenses incurred by the Commission. The FA also announced an even greater punishment by ordering that after serving their suspensions, the seventeen players named in the report would not be allowed to resume playing for Manchester City. Forced to sell the majority of their squad, including the eleven players who had lined up in the 1904 FA Cup final, the club that benefitted most from City's fall from grace was their neighbours Manchester United. Newly promoted to the top tier at the end of season 1905-06, manager Ernest Magnall did not wait to hear the commission's findings and swooped to buy Billy Meredith when Manchester City reacted to the damaging revelations by putting him up for sale. On 16 May, news of a 'Sensational Transfer' was reported in the *Manchester Evening News*:

For reasons which are known to all followers of the game, Meredith did not take part in football last season, and quite a flutter was caused recently when it was announced that the Manchester City Executive had put him on the transfer list, placing the fee for his transfer at the large sum of £500. Many clubs have been desirous of signing him, but Meredith, for personal and other reasons, was not desirous of leaving Manchester.

Having secured the services of the jewel in the crown, Ernest Magnall targeted more players from Manchester City who were due to be sold in November at an auction arranged at the Queen's Hotel in Manchester. Secret negotiations were conducted by Magnall that resulted in the acquisition of two forwards Sandy Turnbull and Jimmy Bannister and also England defender Herbert Burgess. When news of the coup broke, other interested clubs were furious, but, despite protests, the underhand transfers were sanctioned by the FA. While Manchester City would not add anymore silverware for thirty years, lifting the FA Cup in 1934 and the League Championship in 1937, Manchester United's magnificent quartet of new signings formed the backbone of a great team that obtained the club's first major honours gaining the League Championship in 1908 and 1911, the Charity Shield in 1908 and the FA Cup in 1909. An eccentric habit of Billy Meredith's was described in a report of the cup final, settled by a Sandy Turnbull goal against Bristol City, in the *Daily Express*:

Perhaps the most discussed player of the twenty-two was Meredith ... the only footballer who plays with a toothpick in his mouth. It has been hinted that he goes to bed with it. At any rate, it never left his mouth while the game was in progress. He cannot play football without that toothpick, and if Bristol City had been able to obtain possession of it they might have won the game, because Meredith was the most dangerous man against them. Meredith met with several falls on Saturday, but he never relaxed his hold of that piece of quill. ... He was rolling it with his tongue while his comrades were indulging in unrestrained delight at the scoring of the only goal, and when he went to the pavilion to receive his gold medal, he gave Lord Charles Beresford a closer view of it.

A caricature of Billy Meredith chewing his trademark toothpick.

Incredibly, in August 1909, just four months after winning the FA Cup, the entire Manchester United team were banned after forming a trade union. Refusing to sign a new deal, the players were photographed proclaiming their defiance with skipper Charlie Roberts holding a board calling themselves 'The Outcasts FC'. Billy Meredith was at the forefront of the movement and had organised a meeting in Manchester, attended by 500 professional footballers in December 1907, before the FA stamped out the threat by introducing a clause into players contracts disowning the union. Eighteen months on, the United footballers stood firm, and an unnamed player told the *Manchester Evening News*: 'We are fighting for our bread and butter and we shall win too'. Continuing, he went on to say that it had been a 'hard struggle' for many of the team to be 'deprived of their summer

The 'Outcasts FC' who defied authority to form a players' trade union.

pay', but they were 'fighting the battle for the whole of professional footballers of the country' and if they won it would be 'worth the sacrifice'. At the eleventh hour, the FA surprisingly backed down in the face of the agitators and allowed the reimbursement of all lost wages to the suspended players. A truce was declared with the full programme of league matches resuming and the existence of the Players Union fully acknowledged. Despite this significant victory for footballers, the maximum wage was not removed until 1961, when strike action was threatened by the Players Football Association (PFA) led by chairman Jimmy Hill. Billy Meredith did not live to see this change, having died in 1958. PFA secretary Cliff Lloyd visited the destitute octogenarian on his deathbed. As they chatted, Meredith reached under his bed and pulled out a box containing his forty-eight international caps, two league championship medals and two FA Cup winner's medals before summing up his life: 'Always remind your members that those caps and medals didn't look after me in my old age'.

AT THE ELEVENTH HOUR.

PEACE: THERE, MY LAD, PLAY AWAY!

The FA surprisingly acknowledged the existence of the Players Union.

Billy Meredith was bitter that 'caps and medals didn't look after me in my old age'

With his outstanding ability, career longevity and rebellious nature, Billy Meredith was football's first genuine superstar. During a career spanning thirty years, he was nearly thirty-two years old when he moved from City to United and over forty when the league was abandoned for the duration of the First World War, but, remained a top player after hostilities ceased when he was welcomed back into the fold by Manchester City. He made this final move in 1921 and, amazingly, made his last competitive appearance – on the losing side in a FA Cup semi-final – a few months before his 50th birthday in 1924. It's a measure of his greatness and superstar status that he was able to overcome controversy and remain an idol of fans on both sides of the Manchester divide where a popular song was sung on the terraces praising his successful partnership with striker Sandy Turnbull:

> *Oh I wish I was you Billy Meredith*
> *I wish I was you, I envy you, indeed I do!*
> *It ain't that you're tricky with your feet,*
> *But it's those centres that you send in*
> *Which Turnbull then heads in,*
> *Oh, I wish I was you,*
> *Indeed I do!*
> *Indeed I do!*

5
LIFE-BANS FOR MATCH FIXING
1915

*Football is a grand game for developing a
lad physically and morally, for he learns
to play with good temper and unselfishness,
to play in his place and 'play the game',
and these are the best of training
for any game of life.*

Lord Baden-Powell (soldier and founder of the Scout movement)

With the First World War focusing people's minds on battlefields rather than football fields and professional soccer about to be abandoned for the duration, it seemed of little consequence when, on Good Friday, 2 April 1915, relegation-haunted Manchester United secured a vital 2-0 home win against mid-table side Liverpool. A crowd of 15 000 attended Old Trafford in the pouring rain to see a match in which a goal in each half scored by George Anderson gained two vital points for the home side. Jeering from the terraces accompanied a poor spectacle and the *Sporting Chronicle* commented that the visitor's lethargic performance was 'too poor to describe' and the *Liverpool Post* reported, 'A more one sided first half would be hard to witness' while the correspondent of the *Manchester Dispatch* was equally dismissive of the away team's efforts: 'The second half was crammed with lifeless football. United were two up with 22 minutes to

Manchester United won the League Championship in 1911 but were facing relegation in 1915.

play and they seemed so content with their lead that they apparently never tried to increase it. Liverpool scarcely ever gave the impression that they would be likely score'. In fact, Liverpool carved out only two chances to get on the score-sheet. Their captain Pat O'Connell blazed a penalty well-wide and on another occasion, when Fred Pagnam hit the cross-bar, the striker found himself surrounded by angry teammates remonstrating with him. These strange antics fuelled speculation that United's victory had been 'rigged' and it transpired that there had been heavy betting on the match. Unusually for betting patterns of the time, numerous wagers predicting the actual score at odds of up to 8/1 had been placed in several cities including Manchester, Liverpool, Nottingham and London. Bookmaker's suspicions were aroused and a firm known as 'The Football Kings', distributed the following handbill offering a reward for information:

£50 Reward. We have solid grounds for believing that a certain First [Division] League match played in Manchester during Easter weekend was "squared", the home club being permitted to win by a certain score. Further, we have information that several of the players of both teams invested substantial sums on naming the correct score of this match with our firm and others. Such being the case, we wish to inform all our clients and football public generally that we are upholding payment on these correct score transactions, also that we are causing searching investigations to be made with the object of punishing the instigators of this reprehensible conspiracy.

With this object in view we are anxious to receive reliable information bearing on the subject, and we will willingly pay the substantial reward named above to anyone giving which will lead to punishment of the offenders.

When the contents of the handbill were brought to the attention of the Football League, a three-man commission launched an immediate inquiry into the allegations and an appeal for information containing a grim warning for the perpetrators was published in the *Sporting Chronicle*:

We can readily understand the serious unwillingness of bookmakers to be robbed by a conspiracy on the part of players and we are just as determined that League Football shall not be degraded, disgraced, and ruined by such reprehensible practices as referred to in the coupon under notice.

If, as stated therein, direct bets have been made by players, such conduct is contrary to the rules of the FA, and in accordance with declarations by the FA and the Football League, any such player found guilty would be put out of football forever. The conspiracy alleged is a criminal offence upon which the aggrieved parties can take action.

In December, the commission having 'fully investigated the rumours' and received a 'mass of information' published its damning conclusions:

The allegation of squaring the match carried with it a charge of conspiracy by some of the players, and as a result of long and searching investigations we are satisfied that a number of them were party to an arrangement to do so, and joined together to obtain money by betting on the actual result of the match.

Every opportunity has been given to the players to tell the truth, but although they were warned that we were in possession of the facts some have persistently refused to do so, thus revealing a conspiracy to keep back the truth.

The eight-month long investigation revealed that Liverpool footballer, Jackie Sheldon, who was a former Manchester United player, had acted as a go-between and hosted a meeting of some of the participants at the Dog & Partridge public house in Manchester a week before the fixture against Liverpool. The result and score of the forthcoming match was agreed upon and substantial bets were laid to make a quick killing. Along with winger Sheldon, the Liverpool players involved were fullback Bob Purcell, forward Tommy Miller and the unfortunately named halfback Tom Fairfoul. The Manchester culprits were striker Alexander 'Sandy' Turnbull, halfback Arthur Whalley, and forward Enoch 'Knocker' West – although the latter was the only player who actually turned out for United on the day in question. Liverpool's Fred Pagnam, who had done his best to thwart the plan by trying to score a goal, gave evidence against his teammates, as did Manchester United winger Billy Meredith who, insisted he had no previous knowledge of the plot, but soon became suspicious when no one would pass him the ball. The whole sorry episode was summed up in an editorial in the *Athletic News*:

A plot to cheat the public, to sell to the faithful followers of football a sham instead of the genuine article, to rob bookmakers by criminal fraud, and to conspire for the suppression of the truth has been revealed. For the moment the game of Association Football, as played by professionals, staggers under the grave scandal that the League match between Manchester United and Liverpool last Spring was a complete and deliberate fake.

The seven players who were found to have participated in the match-fixing scandal were banned for life and received short shrift from the *Athletic News*:

We have great sympathy with some of those who will have to live under a cloud in that they participated in this hippodrome hocus-pocus and this nefarious contrivance to rob bookmakers who had no chance of preserving their own property. We have not a scrap of compassion for those who have been punished for, not only devising the result of the "match", but for taking from the pockets of bookmakers, who are as much entitled to the protection of the law as other men.

Enoch West always proclaimed his innocence.

Fortunately, for the disgraced players, football administrators were more magnanimous, and, in recognition of their subsequent role as servicemen during the First World War, the bans against six of the seven players were lifted in 1919. Although thirty-eight year old Tom Fairfoul did not return to professional soccer, Jackie Sheldon, Bob Purcell and Tommy Miller resumed their playing careers with Liverpool. Later, Miller even moved to the scene of the crime and enjoyed a spell at Old Trafford. Among the Manchester United players only Arthur Whalley returned to league football. Enoch West had denied any involvement in the scandal and maintained his innocence for the rest of his life. He did not go to war and mounted a legal challenge against the verdict but failed in two attempts to prove a case of libel against his detractors. As a result, the FA did not lift the ban on West until shortly before his 60th birthday in 1945. Sandy Turnbull was posthumously pardoned having lost his life at Arras in France in 1917. Serving with the Eighth Battalion of the East Surrey Regiment, his company was ambushed by a German counter-attack near the village of Chérisey. In a battle involving around 500 'Surreys', 90 were killed, 175 wounded and more than 100 captured. Married with four children, Lance-Sergeant Turnbull was wounded and captured and, with fears for his safety growing, letters were sent to his wife Florence and extracts published in the *Kilmarnock Herald*:

I am writing to try to explain what has happened to your dear husband, Alec. He was wounded, and much to our sorrow, fell into German hands, so I hope you will hear from him. After Alec was wounded he "carried on" and led his men for a mile, playing the game until the last we saw of him. We all loved him, and he was a father to us all and the most popular man in the regiment. All here send our deepest sympathy.

I have very little hope of him being alive. I spoke to him when he got his first wound and asked him if he was badly done. 'No', he said, and from all accounts he must have continued going along with us, and when last seen had four separate wounds.

Sadly, no news was forthcoming about Sandy Turnbull and he was presumed to have died in captivity. The body of the thirty-two year old was never identified and he is one of nearly 35 000 soldiers in the region with an unknown grave whose names are commemorated on the Arras Memorial. Prior to his involvement in the 1915 betting

Sandy Turnbull lost his life serving in the First World War.

scandal, Turnbull had been one of the seventeen players banned after the illegal payments controversy which resulted in his transfer from Manchester City to Manchester United in 1906. A year later, the striker earned notoriety by becoming the first player to be sent off in a Manchester derby after a series of incidents involving his former teammates that were reported in the *Manchester Guardian*: 'Sandy Turnbull (Manchester United) and Manchester City centre-half [Bill] Eadie, made themselves ridiculous early in the game by repeatedly making grimaces at each other, and, in the second half, Turnbull lost control so far as to strike [Joe] Dorsett to the ground. He was promptly ordered off by the referee'. Despite these transgressions, Sandy Turnbull was an integral part of Manchester United's first great side. Under manager Ernest Magnall, he amassed 101 league and cup goals in 247 appearances for Manchester United during a period when the team won the league title in 1908 and 1911. In spite of carrying an injury, Turnbull scored the only goal of the game in the FA Cup final triumph over Bristol City in 1909 when he latched on to a rebound from a shot by Harry Halse that hit the underside of the crossbar. On the Monday following United's cup win, a poetic tribute to Sandy Turnbull was published in the *Athletic News*:

> *Why we thought you were 'crocked' dashing Sandy,*
> *That to fame your road was blocked, Hard Lines Sandy,*
> *But you came up to scratch,*
> *Made the effort for THE match ...*
> *When Halse hit the shiv'ring bar, Lucky Sandy,*
> *There were groans heard near and far, Deep ones, Sandy,*
> *But the ball was on the bound,*
> *And your boot was safe and sound,*
> *When the net your great shot found, Champion Sandy.*

The Football League was suspended during hostilities and when the game returned to normal in 1919, the FA upheld a decision in the aftermath of the match-fixing scandal that, as no official had committed any wrongdoing, the Liverpool and Manchester clubs would not be penalised with fines or

THE GREATER GAME.

A war cartoon in *Punch* reminded professional footballers: "You can make money in this field, but there's only one field where you can get honour"

have points deducted. However, the top division was extended from nineteen to twenty-two clubs in a move that reinstated relegated Chelsea, who had finished second from bottom of the division, above bottom club Tottenham Hotspur and just one point from safety behind Manchester United. In their final last pre-war league game, Chelsea had gained an away point at Goodison Park on 26 April 1915. In this crucial game, their opponents Everton secured the Football League championship in a 2-2 draw. Chelsea's season ended in further disappointment when they were beaten 3-0 by Sheffield United in the FA Cup final – ironically played at Old Trafford. The match was attended by thousands of soldiers – many of whom were recovering from wounds received on the Western Front – and was dubbed the 'Khaki Final'. Due to the war, the final would prove to be virtually the last competitive fixture in England for four years and the importance of abandoning football fields for battlefields was delivered in a stirring patriotic speech by Lord Derby. The *Daily Mirror* reported that after presenting the cup and medals, his lordship addressed the large crowd, proclaiming that now the clubs and their supporters had seen the fate of the FA Cup decided, 'It was now the duty of everyone to join with each other and play a sterner game for England'.

6
PLAYERS' BETTING RING GAOLED
1965

*I have only one complaint about football –
it is the number of 'moaners' in the game…
players who are never satisfied with their
lot and are always wanting something more.
I am being paid well to play a game
I love… That is not much to do for
the money we get!*

Tony Kay (*Charles Buchan's Soccer Gift Book 1962–63*)

Fifty years after the match-fixing scandal involving Manchester City and Liverpool, the soccer world was rocked once again when ten players, including two England internationals, were tried for participating in a match-fixing and fixed-odds betting ring that was described in a newspaper investigation conducted by the *People* as 'The Biggest Sports Scandal of the Century'.

The finale to one of the most shameful episodes in the history of football was played out when prison sentences were passed on the following players in 1965:

Peter Swan (28): centre-half for Sheffield Wednesday and England.

Tony Kay (27): half-back for Sheffield Wednesday, Everton and England.

David 'Bronco' Layne (25): centre-forward for Rotherham, Swindon Town, Bradford City, Mansfield Town and Sheffield Wednesday.

Dick Beattie (27): goalkeeper for Celtic, Portsmouth, Peterborough and St Mirren who also represented the Scottish League and Scotland under 23s.

Brian Philips (32): centre-half for Middlesbrough and Mansfield Town

Ken Thomson (34): centre-half for Aberdeen, Stoke City, Middlesbrough and Hartlepool United.

Ron Howells (29): halfback for Wolverhampton Wanderers, Scunthorpe United, Portsmouth and Walsall.

Sammy Chapman (26): halfback with Mansfield Town and Portsmouth.

Jack Fountain (31): wing-half with Sheffield United, Swindon Town and York City.

Jimmy Gauld (33): former striker with Waterford, St Johnstone, Charlton, Everton, Plymouth, Swindon and Mansfield.

The spider at the centre of a web of deceit was Jimmy Gauld, a one-time Scotland youth international and journeyman striker, whose travels had taken him to clubs in the Irish League, Scottish League and Football League. In August 1959, Swindon paid a then club record fee of £7000 to buy Gauld from Plymouth Argyle. After Swindon had entertained Mansfield in February 1960, some of the players from both sides had dinner together and agreed to participate in fixed-odds betting by deliberately losing the forthcoming fixtures Swindon v Port Vale and

Ringleader Jimmy Gauld boasted he was making £1000 a week from the betting scam.

Mansfield v Tranmere Rovers. Accurately 'forecasting' the results of multiple matches could yield handsome profits from bookmakers and the scheme escalated when Gauld was transferred from Swindon to Mansfield in November 1960. The striker's playing days were numbered when he suffered the tragedy of a broken leg the following month. Whilst fighting a long losing battle to regain fitness (for which he subsequently received an insurance pay-out of £500 from the Professional Footballers Association), he utilised his widespread contacts in the game to fix results over a network of fixtures from Dundee in the north to Exeter in the south; Ipswich in the east to Swindon in the west; Oldham in the north-west to Hartlepool in the north-east; Portsmouth in the south-east to Bristol in the south-west. Bookmakers became suspicious about the amount of betting on shock results and Jimmy Gauld's greed contributed to his ultimate downfall when he lodged a formal complaint to Ladbrokes when the firm refused to pay him his winnings. An investigation ensued and in November 1961, Alan Hardaker, secretary of the Football League, interviewed Gauld who admitted his involvement in fixed-odds gambling but denied any wrong-doing. Despite being warned that his conduct was being closely scrutinised, Gauld continued his illegal activities until the scheme unravelled in March 1963 when Bristol Rovers goalkeeper Esmond Million broke down and confessed to his manager after an abject display in which he had blatantly given away two goals in a match against Bradford Park Avenue. Suspended by his club and his playing career in tatters, Million sold his story to the *People* and named several other players involved in the scam. A series of magistrates hearings followed in which a number of footballers were fined for their involvement in the betting ring. Ultimately, Jimmy Gauld appeared before Rochdale Magistrates in October 1963 to answer six charges of offering bribes to footballers and was fined £10 on each count. With the net closing in, Gauld decided to go public and, on the same day he left court, approached the *People* claiming that his betting ring earned him £1000 a week and boasted that there was 'a queue of players wanting to join the scheme'. Before the newspaper serialised the sensational story in April 1964, the editor demanded conclusive proof of the allegations and investigative journalists watched the crooked informant as he called at the houses of co-conspirators. Players were lured into his car on some pretext, unaware that the ensuing conversations about their illegal transactions were being secretly recorded on a machine placed under the seat. One of Gauld's interviews with Everton's Tony Kay confirmed that one of the big clubs had been tainted with the involvement of two teammates at his former club Sheffield Wednesday. David Layne had recruited Kay and Swan after an unplanned meeting with Gauld whom he had played with at Mansfield. The trio won £100 each after conspiring to bet on their own side losing to struggling Ipswich Town on 1 December 1962. On the same day, Gauld arranged for two other matches to result in home wins, Lincoln City v Brentford and York City v Oldham Athletic. Peter Swan later testified that he invested £50 after Layne told him he 'knew some games which were going to be fixed and he could get me two-to-one odds'.

Press interest reached fever pitch when ten footballers from all four divisions were committed for trial with the prospect of prison sentences at Nottingham Assizes in January 1965. The court heard that Jack Fountain, who had known Gauld at Swindon, before joining York City, was the first to assist Gauld, followed by former Mansfield captains Sammy Chapman and Brian Phillips. As the enterprise grew, Gauld and his contacts recruited Dick Beattie, Ken Thomson, Ron Howells, David Layne and Tony Kay. Peter Swan, capped nineteen times by England, saw Jimmy Gauld for the first time when they stood together in the dock, having sacrificed his international career and his reputation for winnings of a paltry £100.

In mitigation, defence counsel for goalkeeper Dick Beattie explained that there was a great deal of 'unrest' and an 'unsavoury atmosphere' among professional footballers concerning the low pay they received for entertaining huge crowds. This statement referred to the fact that, before the maximum wage was abolished in 1961, no British player earned more than £20 a week during the season with bonuses of £2 for a win and £1 for a draw. Fulham and England captain Johnny Haynes subsequently became the first British player to earn £100 a week (worth around £2,000 today, although this figure falls well short of the £300 000 a week paid to current Manchester United and England captain Wayne

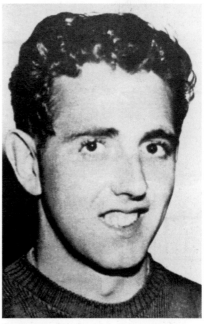

Goalkeeper Dick Beattie's defence lawyer talked of 'unrest' over the low pay of professional footballers.

Rooney), but the highest paid defendant, Tony Kay, received a basic wage of only £45 a week from Everton – who had paid a club record transfer fee of £56 000 for his signature – before he helped them to top the First Division and win the League Championship trophy in 1963. The majority of defendants who plied their trade in the lower divisions were on an average of £22 a week. It transpired that Ken Thomson had come to the end of his playing career and placed a bet purely to fund his training as a student teacher at Durham University. The trial judge, Mr Justice Lawton, had some sympathy with the assessment of the players' finances: 'It has occurred to me, having seen the procession of footballers in the box during

Ken Thomson and his wife Doreen ran a newsagent's shop while he was at Stoke City. His downfall began when he placed a bet to fund a teacher training course.

this case that they are not all that highly paid'. However, this submission could not be accepted as an excuse for corruption and the judge had no hesitation in passing custodial sentences on all ten defendants: Jack Fountain and Brian Philips were jailed for 15 months; Dick Beattie for nine months; Ken Thomson, Ron Howells and Sammy Chapman for six months; David Layne, Tony Kay and Peter Swan were dealt with relatively lightly receiving four months imprisonment. Sentencing the England internationals Peter Swan and Tony Kay, the judge said, 'You present me with the most unpleasant part of my duty. I accept you were involved on one isolated occasion and I accept it was really by chance you got involved – the chance of Layne going to Mansfield to watch a football match on a day of relaxation. On the other hand, Kay and Swan as internationals should have been able to protect themselves against any blandishments held out. The greater your distinction in football the greater your fall must be'. The following season, Layne, Kay and Swan would be unavailable for

Britain's first £100 a week footballer Johnny Haynes is chaired off the field by Jimmy Armfield and Peter Swan (left) following England's record 9-3 victory over Scotland at Wembley in 1961.

selection when Sheffield Wednesday lost a five goal thriller against Everton in the 1966 FA Cup final. Two months later, Kay and Swan missed out again, having thrown away their chance of being considered for the England squad that lifted the World Cup at Wembley.

The heaviest punishment in the dramatic match-fixing trial was reserved for ringleader Jimmy Gauld whose own counsel conceded he had 'acted as a Judas and betrayed others'. Pleading guilty to fourteen counts of 'conspiracy to defraud', the court heard that Gauld had made £3275 from betting on fixed matches and been paid a fee of £7240 by the *People* newspaper. Jailing him for four years and ordering him to pay £5000 costs, trial judge Mr Justice Lawton described the defendant as an 'unpleasant rogue' and spoke of the deception that had affected thousands of ordinary supporters who had unwittingly paid to watch a 'dishonest charade':

Your crime has been great. It is my duty to pass a sentence on you to make it clear to all evil-minded people in all branches of sport that this activity is a crime and a serious crime. Over a long period and from one end of this kingdom to another you have befouled professional football and corrupted your friends and acquaintances. You have done it to put money in your own pocket. You are responsible for the ruin of footballers of the distinction of Kay and Swan and you have ruined the life of an intelligent man like Thomson. This is not the end. I have to look at the public consequences of your behaviour. I have got to think of the young footballers who came into football in the years you were operating your criminal enterprises and the example and those associated with you gave these young men... I have reminded myself time and time again during this trial that I am not sitting here as a committee of the Football Association condemning people for breaking the rules and to condemn those who behaved in the way you behaved when you sold the reputations of your friends to the People *newspaper.*

Football League secretary Alan Hardaker, conceded that for every one of the thirty-three footballers fined or jailed during the course of the investigation, there were probably twenty more who had escaped punishment. The players brought before the courts were banned *sine die* by the Football Association, although this decision was later revised and seven years later the players were allowed to appeal. By 1972, most were too old to make a comeback and Ken Thomson had died having suffered a heart attack on a golf course at the age of thirty-nine in 1969. Former First Division footballers, David Layne and Peter Swan were offered the chance to resurrect their careers at Sheffield Wednesday. While Layne failed to progress beyond the reserves, and made only four league appearances whilst on loan with Hereford United, thirty-four year old Swan made an emotional return to the

Tony Kay's descent into crime culminated in an offer he couldn't refuse from the Krays.

first team, making fifteen Second Division appearances for 'The Owls'. Moving on to Bury at the end of the season, he captained 'The Shakers' to promotion from the Fourth Division to the Third Division in 1973–74, then retired from playing and enjoyed managerial success leading Matlock Town to victory in the FA Challenge Trophy at Wembley in 1975. Meanwhile, Tony Kay had fallen foul of the law once again and he fled abroad to avoid arrest after selling a fake diamond ring. During a twelve year exile in Spain, he crept back to England and, while visiting friends, was arrested and fined £400 on the outstanding warrant. Tony Kay later recalled that following his release from prison in 1965, he had received a first class rail ticket and an offer 'I didn't dare refuse' to travel to London. There he was entertained and questioned, about the procedure concerning the controversial admission of taped evidence at his trial, by the notorious gangland brothers – 'The Krays'.

7
THE MURDER TRIAL OF AN FA CUP HERO
1916

Sandy Young's case is deserving of practical sympathy as well as condemnation. The Football Hero has far greater temptation put in his way than any ordinary man, just as the star turn has in other walks of life.

Stud Marks, *The Argus*, August 1916

In the first half of the Twentieth Century, Everton FC were blessed with three great strikers who graced the No.9 jersey and won major honours with the club, Dixie Dean, Tommy Lawton and their predecessor, Sandy Young – the goal hero of the 1906 FA Cup final at Crystal Palace where Everton defeated Newcastle United.

The Everton frontman scored the only goal of the final converting a cross from winger Jack Sharp who, by common consent, was the 'man of the match'. A superb all-round sportsman, Sharp shares with Everton and Lancashire CCC teammate Harry Makepeace the rare distinction of having played both football and cricket at full international level for England. The

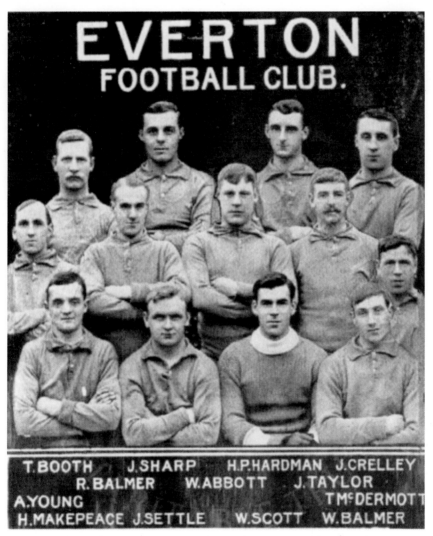

The Everton squad in 1906.

soccer correspondent of the *Times* reported that the 'hard grounds and high temperatures common to April and totally unsuited to a winter game' had contributed to a disappointing final tie on this showpiece occasion:

The footballers played a disjointed, hard-kicking game that possessed neither art nor efficacy. Neither side ever found the consistent swing for its game; and a good deal of the match was a mere kicking duel between the half and full backs. Luck did the rest, and was mostly on the side of Everton. In the whole of the 90 minutes' play there were not half-a-dozen hard shots, indeed about four was nearer the mark. There was really only piece of concentrated judgement and execution, and this yielded the one goal of the match, which was scored by Young from a centre by Sharp, when the game had lasted an hour and a quarter. The football was a mere lottery from beginning to end. The chances went mostly Everton's way, but even Everton relied only on its one bit of real football to win.

The poor standard of football did not concern the followers of Everton, who having suffered the disappointment of seeing their team lose in two previous finals (against Wolverhampton Wanderers in 1893 and Aston Villa in 1897) concluded that 'the third time counts for all'. A headline in the *Liverpool Football Echo* triumphantly announced, 'Cup Comes to Liverpool at Last' and likened the eruption that greeted the winning goal to the devastating earthquake that had occurred earlier that week in San Francisco. Two years earlier the *Illustrated Sporting and Dramatic News* had written a glowing appraisal of Sandy Young recounting how the striker had overcome long periods out of the game due to 'feeble health' before returning to form that led them to 'confidently anticipate' that 'he will leave behind all his previous records in the matter of goal scoring, and we trust that he will have the pleasure of wearing either an Association Cup or League Championship medal'. Acknowledging, that with a slight physique, standing 5 feet 8 inches in height and weighing just over 11 stone, Young was not the 'battering-ram species' of centre-forward but a player who chose 'to exhibit some degree of cleverness in originality and execution', the article paid tribute to his intelligent style and, whatever the provocation, unfailing good sportsmanship:

A contemporary illustration of Jack Sharp's cross to Sandy Young which produced the winning goal for Everton in the 1906 FA Cup final.

Young has a capital idea of centre-forward play and under certain conditions can wreak havoc on an opposing defence. He is one of a class of footballer who depends upon skill to produce effect, and mere physical force is a nonentity as far as his methods are concerned. ... In distributing the play to his wings Young has few superiors, and a centre-half who confines his attention to the ball finds in him a most troublesome opponent. Whether success attends his efforts or not, he enters into the spirit of every game, takes his hard knocks in the true stoical fashion, and ever and anon coming up with the same pleasant smile and good-humoured intent. Like every footballer, he has his off days, and what individual is there that can boast of the contrary? When seen at his best, Young can give a long start to the majority of centre-forwards in the country, and we have seen him in deadly form near goal.

Sandy Young was not the 'battering ram' type of striker.

Alexander 'Sandy' Young was born in Slamannan, Stirlingshire in 1880. His football career started with Falkirk and St Mirren before he moved South and joined Everton in 1901. At Goodison Park he became an international footballer twice capped for Scotland. Bringing the FA Cup to Merseyside for the first time was the crowning glory of Young's playing record that realised 124 goals in 314 League and FA Cup matches. A year after scoring the only goal of the game in the 1906 cup final, the prolific marksman became the English First Division's top scorer with a haul of twenty-eight goals. Having served the 'Toffees' with distinction for ten years, many fans were upset the club's record goal-scorer was not re-signed and threatened to boycott Goodison Park. A supporter submitted the following tribute to the striker's contribution which was published in the *Liverpool Echo*:

I have been a regular attender at Everton matches since the days of [Alec] Dick and [George] Dobson in the 1880s and I unhesitatingly affirm that Sandy Young is the greatest forward that has played under the club's colours. Young has been and is the club's greatest asset.

Despite the protests Sandy Young moved on and had brief unproductive spells with Tottenham Hotspur and Manchester City in 1911, before winding down his playing career with South Liverpool and Port Vale. Sandy Young had invested in the future by making a loan of £150 to his elder married brother John who purchased a farm in Australia at Tongala, a small township in Northern Victoria. In May 1914, Sandy migrated to join his brother and advanced further sums of £75 and £100. The monies were not repaid and the brothers' relationship deteriorated into a series of increasingly violent quarrels. On 30 November 1915, the simmering feud was witnessed by a friend who visited the brothers and saw an argument that ended with Sandy threatening to take control of the farm, 'What about those cows, half of them belong to me' protested John. 'I don't think so', countered Sandy, 'my cheque paid for them'. As the friend left, Sandy told him, 'I cannot stop here, I'm afraid John will murder me'. Likewise, John pleaded, 'Don't go away yet, I am afraid that Alex will come out and shoot me'. John's chilling prophecy came true a day later in an incident on 1 December, in which John was shot dead by Sandy who then turned the weapon on himself and suffered a superficial cheek wound in a forlorn attempt to commit suicide. In what was to become known as the 'Tongala Tragedy', one local newspaper, the *Rivine Herald* described the affair as 'a tragedy unequalled in the history of the district'. As he lay dying in Echuca Hospital, John Young made a statement: 'I was milking a cow, when Alexander came up and said, "I am going to shoot you". I replied, "Put the gun away. You are only trying to frighten me". Alexander however, took no notice, and fired at me". Sandy Young listened to his brother's deathbed testimony and agreed at the time that this version of the shooting was correct, and in a statement before a justice of the peace testified, 'I went to the shed to shoot my brother. When I told him that I was going to shoot him he said, "Go on" and of course I fired'.

However, when facing charges of 'wilful murder', during his trial at Bendigo Supreme Court in June 1916, the defendant denied any knowledge of either hearing his brother's allegation or making an incriminating statement at the hospital. Trial judge Mr Justice Cussen presided over a hushed court as Sandy Young took the witness stand and told the jury that he had not 'got on' with his brother who threatened him on several occasions. The deceased had hit him on the head with a bucket and on the body with a stick. In another incident John had chased him brandishing a pitch fork and also threatened to shoot him. On the night before the tragedy his brother attacked him without provocation, striking him on the head and arm with a stick. John said, 'You or me will have to enter heaven tonight'. Early, next morning he had heard a noise in the house and thought it was his brother. Getting out of bed, he took his gun and loaded it. Carrying the gun to the shed where his brother was milking cows, he asked him if he had been in the house. John replied, 'No'. Sandy then brought up the thorny question of the loans and demanded, 'What about my money?' Whereupon his brother picked up a shovel and threatened to hit him. Sandy took flight and his brother chased him for about forty yards, before he stopped and, turning to face his brother warned, 'Stand or I will fire'. John, however, proceeded to attack him with the shovel, forcing him to open fire in self-defence. John Young fell, and Sandy, picking up the shovel, carried it to the house, where he placed the gun against his face and shot himself. He did not remember anything subsequently until a week later when he recovered in the Echuca Hospital.

Mr Justice Cussen posed a pertinent question to the defendant, 'Why did you try to blow your brains out when you considered you had only shot your brother in self-defence'. To which Young replied, 'I cannot say'. The jury retired to consider the verdict and, after deliberating for an hour, returned a verdict of 'Not guilty' on the charge of murder but regarded that the accused man was 'Guilty' on the lesser charge of manslaughter. Young was remanded in custody to await sentence. Six months earlier, at a meeting of the Everton Board in January 1916, Sandy Young's predicament was discussed and the directors resolved to send a cable 'intimating that we could testify to Young's mental unsoundness'. The *Liverpool Echo* commented that Young had a 'curious temperament' and was 'highly strung' with 'peculiar habits'. Furthermore, he was a 'sombre man' who 'would live alone' and many a time 'no one could get a word out of him'. He was often to be seen stroking the single lock of hair that adorned his forehead which 'suggested he suffered severe pains in his head'. Recognising the relevance of these behavioural problems, Everton wrote to the Mayor of Tongala saying that they 'can and desire to submit medical and other testimony to prove that Young is and has been mentally unsound'. This intervention was taken into consideration by the court and a remarkably light sentence of three years imprisonment was passed. The defendant made an appeal to

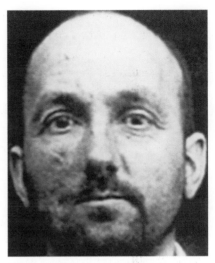

Prisoner 34341 Alexander Young in July 1916.

Everton and the citizens of Liverpool to make donations to settle his £200 legal bill and shortly before he was released from Ararat Lunatic Asylum, he contacted his former club for further financial assistance and received £20 from the directors. A colourful rumour circulated suggesting that Sandy Young was later hanged for cattle rustling, but the truth is less prosaic. Released in 1919, he sailed back home in May 1920 and lived the life of a recluse in Scotland. Apart from occasionally contacting Everton for money, how he conducted the remainder of his life remains largely a mystery. In September 1959, at the age of 79, he died in a mental institution in Edinburgh. Buried in a pauper's grave, this state of affairs was rectified by Everton Heritage Society who funded a new headstone at Seafield Cemetery on the seafront at Edinburgh. At a poignant ceremony in March 2015, a lone piper played a rendition of 'Grand Old Team'. Former Everton and Scotland heroes Graeme Sharp, Graham Stuart and Sandy's namesake, Alex 'The Golden Vision' Young were in attendance, standing at the graveside alongside descendants of the Young family. Amongst them was Sandy Young's nephew, eighty-seven year old Cyril Cleeton, who during

Namesake Alex Young was among the former Everton heroes who attended the ceremony for a new headstone on the grave of Sandy Young.

his childhood had once shaved his uncle with a single-edge razor in the little cottage in Westfield, West Lothian, where his uncle lived as a recluse after returning from Australia: 'I had no idea he was such a good footballer. I knew he had once played for Falkirk and Everton, but Everton played in a different country – we had no idea he was held in such high esteem. He didn't talk about it'. Cyril realised there was something else he his uncle didn't want to talk about: 'While I was shaving him I noticed a deep gouge on his right cheek. "What happened there?" He just said, "We don't mention that". Of course, it was the mark left when he tried to shoot himself after killing his brother'.

A happier memory relating to Sandy Young's football career and his famous FA Cup final goal for Everton was recalled in verse published on the back of a service sheet produced for the graveside ceremony:

As sweet as toffee to the tongue,
Was that one splendid goal by Young.

7
THE MURDER OF A FOOTBALLER
1923

Abide with me; fast falls the eventide;
The darkness deepens; Lord, with me abide;
Where is death's sting?
Where, grave, thy victory?
I triumph still, if Thou abide with me.

Rev. Henry Francis Lyte (writer of football's first anthem)

On Armistice Day 1923, a former soldier who had seen service under Lord Kitchener in the Sudan and been invalided out of the army after being wounded and gassed in the First World War, fired a shotgun to commit the apparently motiveless killing of his neighbour and tenant, Tommy Ball. The high profile victim was a central defender with leading club Aston Villa and his untimely death brought him the unfortunate distinction of being the only British professional footballer who has been proved to have been murdered.

On the day before the incident that claimed his life Tommy Ball made his 74th league appearance in Aston Villa's 1-0 away win over Notts County and the result lifted the Midland club to third position in the old First Division. Considered a brilliant prospect, twenty-three year old Ball was born in Chester-le-Street, County Durham and his soccer talent was recognised whilst playing for Wadley Colliery. In the grand north-east working class tradition that a football scout only had to whistle down a coal-pit to sign a professional footballer, Tommy Ball had a spell with Newcastle United reserves before moving to Aston Villa in January 1920. Three months later, he made his league debut at right-back, deputising for double international footballer and cricketer Andy Ducat, who had captained the 'Villains' to victory over Huddersfield Town in the 1920 FA Cup final, before establishing himself in the team at centre-half following the transfer to Manchester United of the legendary England international, Frank Barson, a controversial character renowned as the 'most suspended

Andy Ducat receiving the FA Cup in 1920.

man ever' who was rumoured to have once pulled a gun on members of the Villa management committee and would end his career by being sent off in his own benefit match!

In stark contrast to the volatile 'hard man' Frank Barson, Tommy Ball was considered to have a good temperament whose play was scrupulously fair. Powerfully built, commanding in the air and strong in the tackle, the *Birmingham Gazette* would remember him as 'one of the most popular players of the day' and went on to say: 'Few men in his position were more feared by opposing attackers, on the other hand, few men were more popular with their foes... A pluckier player never stepped on the field. He has gone through more than one hard game with injuries which would have put many a player out for several days'.

Tommy Ball married the daughter of a local butcher, Beatrice Richards, in May 1922 and on the evening she was to become a widow, the couple left

their home shortly before 8pm and went out for a drink at the Church Tavern. Arriving there at 8.30pm, Mrs Ball drank one glass of stout while her husband had a Stone's ginger and three halves of mild ale. When the pub closed an hour later at 9.30pm (a legacy of wartime restrictions), the couple spent a few minutes in cordial conversation with the licensee outside the tavern before catching the bus on the Walsall Road which dropped them off near their home in Brick Kiln Lane, Perry Bar. Tommy Ball and his wife had rented their home in January 1923 from George Stagg, a forty-five year old former soldier

Aston Villa's Tommy Ball was shot dead outside his home.

and police officer. The property landlord had joined the Royal Warwickshire Regiment in 1895 and during the next nine years served in campaigns in Egypt and the Sudan, before joining the Birmingham Police Force and serving as a constable for ten years before answering the call to arms and resuming military service at the outbreak of the First World War in 1914. Serving in France with the Seaforth Highlanders, Stagg was shot though the calf of his left leg and gassed during the Battle of Neuve Chapelle. Invalided out of the army in 1916, Stagg was deemed unfit to resume his career in the police force and was granted a small pension. Married with four children, the teetotal war veteran worked in various factories until he had in his own words, 'scraped and saved' enough to buy two properties known as Somerville Cottages in Brick Lane.

Tensions had been rising between landlord and tenants over the garden area outside the adjoining cottages. Each of the properties had a gate but the gardens were only separated by a small wall. The Balls kept chickens which continually wandered on to Stagg's land. Tommy Ball had attempted to solve the problem by penning the fowl up in one of two unused pigsties in the garden, but Stagg had objected to this, arguing that the Balls had no right to use the sties that belonged to him. The situation came to a head in August when Stagg gave the Balls notice to quit saying angrily, 'The fowls are a nuisance, you all ought to be poisoned'. However, despite their willingness to leave, the unwanted tenants had failed to find alternative accommodation and three months later, the situation erupted with fatal consequences on Sunday 11 November 1923. Armistice Day had started peacefully enough with George Stagg obliging his tenant by collecting and delivering a Sunday newspaper, but that evening, after returning from his local, Tommy Ball went outside to look for his dog as his wife prepared supper at 10.30pm. George Stagg's dog was also outside in a kennel and when it began barking, its annoyed owner, strode out of his house into the garden carrying a loaded single-barrelled shotgun. Following a verbal exchange between the two men, Stagg suddenly fired a warning shot then, reloaded and fired again, this time Tommy Ball was struck in the body. Beatrice Ball ran outside and saw the mortally wounded footballer clutching his chest. The victim staggered towards his wife and cried out with his dying breath, 'Oh, Beat! He has shot me!' Mrs Ball's clothes became covered in blood and she screamed as she thought she felt the wind from a bullet as it passed over her shoulder. Panic stricken she called for help and her landlord appeared from his house and said, 'It's only me Mrs Ball. Don't be afraid. I haven't hurt you have I?' He then tried to explain that the shooting of her husband had been an accident and she replied, 'It could not have been an accident or you would not have fired at me'. As Stagg's wife Mary looked on from a bedroom window, the gunman assisted Beatrice to carry her dead husband inside the Balls house and lay the body on a couch. A doctor was called and pronounced Tommy Ball dead from a wound through the heart measuring the size of a 'half-crown' coin (3mm in diameter). The police arrived to investigate and Sergeant Davenport arrested and charged George Stagg with 'wilful murder'. When questioned at West Bromwich police station, the prisoner insisted that the incident had been nothing more than a tragic accident explaining that he had gone outside with the weapon when he heard someone entering his garden and fired the gun to frighten the intruder away and that the gun had discharged as the pair grappled over it: 'I immediately went out and done all I could for him. I helped to pick him up and put him on the sofa, and immediately went for the doctor, and informed the first police officer I met'.

At the trial of George Stagg at Stafford Assizes in February 1924, the defendant gave evidence and tried to blacken his victim's character by claiming that he had regularly seen Tommy Ball 'kicking his wife about' and furthermore, his victim was 'frequently under the influence' and the worse the wear for drink on the night of the argument when the gun was accidently discharged when he fell backwards during the struggle. Beatrice Ball returned to the witness box and vehemently denied the allegations of wife-beating and drunkenness. Significantly, the only other witness to the night's events, Mary Stagg who, as the dead man lay in the garden had shouted at Ball's wife, 'You are a lot of night bowlers', reserved the right not to give evidence at the trial of her husband. In his testimony to the court, George Stagg gave his version of the tragic events:

Aston Villa skipper Frank Moss shakes hands with Frank Hudspeth before the 1924 FA Cup final.

There was no malice or aforethought. It was quite an accident. My dog was barking as Ball went past my garden gate and he was shouting to the dog to stop it. I jumped out of my chair in which I had been dozing. I told my dog to go in, and Ball, who was under the influence of drink, shouted to me: 'Go in and go to bed or I will bash your brains out'. I said, 'Now, Tom, go in and go to bed. There's a good chap'. Mrs Stagg was up at the window, having gone to bed, and shouted from the window: 'Go in and don't make a noise to wake the children'. Ball shouted to Mrs Stagg: 'I will bash your brains out', and went to climb over the garden gate. The gate was latched and bolted. I had the gun in my hand when I went to the gate to see what was the matter was because the dog was barking. I told him to get off the gate and go to bed and used the gun to frighten him. He went away and came back again and tried to get over the gate again. I pushed him back with the muzzle of the gun, and he caught hold of the gun and tried to wrench it from me. As I wrenched the gun away I stepped back and the gun went off – a sudden jerk and off it went'.

The Judge in his summing up advised the jury that their verdict came down to a simple choice, 'If death was caused by the gun being pointed at the man and discharged on purpose, that was murder. If it went off by accident during a struggle it was manslaughter'. The jury retired for an absence of 100 minutes and delivered a 'guilty' verdict of 'wilful murder'. The judge donned the black cap and passed the death sentence on George Stagg. A month later, the defence team failed in an attempt to obtain leave to appeal to overturn the murder conviction and substitute it with a verdict of manslaughter. However, the Home Secretary acted on the jury's recommendation for mercy and reprieved the condemned murderer who spent the remainder of his life in custody. Three years into his sentence he was declared insane and transferred to Broadmoor and spent time in a variety of mental institutions before dying at Highcroft Mental Hospital in Birmingham aged eighty-seven in February 1966.

The tragedy robbed Tommy Ball of the opportunity of making an appearance at Wembley in a meeting between his former clubs Aston Villa and Newcastle, which resulted in a victory for the 'Magpies' in the final of

Villa players past and present attended the victim's funeral.

the FA Cup in 1924. Aston Villa's next home game following the death of Tommy Ball was an emotional affair, not least for Vic Milne, an amateur player and qualified doctor, wearing the number 5 shirt previously donned by the murder victim. As a sign of respect, the flag above Villa Park was lowered to half-mast, both teams wore black armbands, and a collection taken around the ground raised £127 (the modern equivalent of £6700) for the widow of the dead footballer. Two days

One of the footballs adorning each corner of the grave was donated as a 'token of esteem' by the former colleagues of Tommy Ball.

later, on Monday 19 November, first team players attended their former teammate's funeral and crowds lined the route as the cortège journeyed to St John's Parish Church where Tommy Ball was laid to rest. Among the wreaths was the offering of the Villa team consisting of a large square of moss representing a football ground with yellow and white chrysanthemums worked into the shape of a football and on either side were draped the club colours of claret and blue. The grave was lined with evergreens and the gravestone took the form of a granite imitation football atop a stone plinth with stone footballs adorning each corner of the grave. Around the edge of the grave was inscribed the following text: 'Saith the Lord: Justice and Mercy is Given Only in the Kingdom of Heaven'.

Author FR Gittins composed a poetical summary of the tragedy that had befallen the much missed sportsman:

Memorial Poem of Thomas Ball

'Twas on a Sabbath Evening
In drear November days,
Two friends were heard "Creating"
In Perry Barr's byways
High words just fed the anger
The young man's life is fled
A shot and then another!
And Thomas Ball was dead!!!

Tis sad to think of her now left
Alone to fight in "life"
Without Protector's kindest care
Of husband unto Wife.
Though Fame was His
And cash not short,
They proved alas in vain,

And Aston Villa lose a man,
Who always played the game.

Of poor Stagg's fate nought can we say
The Law impels to silence,
The motive too is quite obscure
Until they break the Seal.
And lonely hearts the wide world o'er
Will pity all concerned,
In this sad tragedy near Brum
Of which we have just learned.
Requiescat in Pace.

9
THE BOGOTA BRACELET INCIDENT
1970

*If you can meet with triumph and disaster
and treat these imposters just the same...*

Rudyard Kipling (author of soccer's favourite poem *If*)

During the 'Swinging Sixties', Bobby Moore was the golden boy of English football as he achieved a unique treble by captaining teams to three major trophies in three consecutive years at Wembley Stadium. In 1964, his club, West Ham defeated Preston North End to win the FA Cup and built on this feat to clinch the European Cup Winners' Cup against TSV Munich in 1965, then, in the national side, alongside two of his club teammates Martin Peters and Geoff Hurst, Moore skippered England to victory against West Germany in the final of the 1966 World Cup.

Having been recognised by the Football Writers Association who voted him 'Footballer of the Year' in 1964, Bobby Moore became the first footballer to win the BBC Sports Personality of the Year award two years later and also topped a poll of 600 journalists among the world's press who voted him 'Player of Players' at the 1966 World Cup. For their part in England's triumph, manager Alf Ramsey was honoured with a knighthood and his on-field lieutenant Bobby Moore received an OBE. As reigning champions, England were not required to qualify in group matches for the

Bobby Moore receives the World Cup from Queen Elizabeth in 1966.

1970 World Cup in Mexico and supporters were optimistic about retaining the Jules Rimet trophy, typified in this verse by housewife Ann Smith that appeared in an edition of *Charles Buchan's Football Monthly*:

> *To Manager Alf Ramsey, just four more years to go,*
> *Then another bid to win that cup in far-off Mexico.*
> *Three cheers for Merry England, for courage, nerve and skill;*
> *The game which England first made great – has made her greater still.*

Pele once nominated Bobby Moore as the 'greatest' defender of them all.

The great Brazilian footballer Pele once paid the England captain the ultimate compliment: 'Of the hundreds of defenders that played against me during my career, I pick Bobby Moore as the greatest of them all. He was very determined but always fair, and a wonderful ambassador for English football'. Significantly, Moore's role as a sporting 'ambassador' came under severe scrutiny when he became embroiled in an international scandal during an acclimatisation tour in South America prior to the World Cup finals in 1970. The infamous incident occurred after the England squad flew to Colombia and defeated the national team 4-0 in a warm-up game. Whilst relaxing in England's Tequendama Hotel in Bogota, Bobby Moore and Bobby Charlton visited the Feugo Verde (Green Fire) jewellery store in the hotel lobby. Bobby Charlton later recounted how he was interested in buying a ring he saw on display for his wife and asked the shop assistant if he could see it: 'The young woman took the ring out of the cabinet and brought it round to us. She had taken it out having first opened a door. We discussed the price, or I should say we worked it out, and found it was too expensive so we left. We had been in the shop

Bobby Charlton won the Footballer of the Year award before taking part in England's World Cup triumph in 1966.

five minutes at most'. The two players then strolled across the hotel foyer and sat down on seats opposite the shop window. Moore explained what happened next: 'We were just chatting idly. I watched an elderly woman go into the shop, come out again and walk towards us. She asked me and Bobby to step into the shop. We said, "Yes", thinking they had something to interest Bobby for his wife. As we stood up the woman fumbled with the cushions where we'd been sitting. Still nothing registered. But as we got back inside the shop she said: "There's some jewellery missing"'. The shocked players immediately volunteered to be searched but the offer was rejected and the police were called instead. Manager Alf Ramsey was informed and both players made formal statements before the matter was seemingly closed. England then journeyed to Ecuador for a further friendly match. When they returned to Bogota, to change planes en-route to Mexico on 25 May, armed police met the flight and Bobby Moore was sensationally arrested on charges of stealing a gold bracelet studded with emeralds valued at £600. The England party were forced to depart without their captain and key defender who remained behind to face the music supported by two senior FA officials, secretary Denis Follows and chairman, Dr Andrew Stephens. A major diplomatic row developed as British Prime Minister Harold Wilson sent a telegram to President of the FA, Lord Harewood, saying: 'We were all greatly concerned to hear the news about Bobby Moore… Our embassy will do everything they can to help solve this matter as speedily as possible and to safeguard Bobby Moore's interests and welfare'. The First Secretary of the British Embassy in Bogota lost no time in lodging a formal protest to the Colombian Foreign Minister and the legal services of Senor Vicente Laverde, a former Colombian Minister of Justice, were retained to represent Moore, who was placed under house arrest and shadowed by two armed guards at the hacienda of Alfonso Senior, director of the Colombian Football Federation. In addition to seeking retribution for the theft of the £600 bracelet, the owner of the jewellery shop, Danilo Rojas, also claimed £4000 in 'moral and material damages'. Gradually, the case against Moore began to unravel when it emerged that other visiting celebrities in the city, such as singers and bullfighters, had been similarly 'set-up' for the purpose of extortion and had caved into demands for money to avoid adverse publicity. Sir Alf Ramsey was normally reticent, but sprang to the defence of his team captain saying that he did not believe that the allegation of theft had been a simple 'misunderstanding' but was a case of 'someone wanting to achieve notoriety out of the England soccer team. This sort of thing has happened in the same place [Colombia] several times before. The authorities are aware of this'. In fact, Brazil manager, Joao Saldanha, later confided to Moore that he had once been set-up in similar fashion in Colombia, but had reacted quickly to the situation and locked the doors of the shop, called the police and insisted that he was searched.

Two days after his unexpected detention the England captain was brought face to face with his accusers at a reconstruction held at the scene of the 'crime' where scores of onlookers gathered outside the shop. Judge Pedro Dorado heard salesgirl Clara Padilla testify that she had seen Moore toying with a wall-mounted display case before stealing the bracelet and putting it in his pocket. She also accused two other players, Bobby Charlton and someone else she did not recognise, of being accomplices to the theft. A dubious passer-by was produced, Alvaro Suarez, claiming to have witnessed the incident from outside the window where he saw the accused reach into the cabinet and help himself to the bracelet. The police established that the footballer's hand was too large to remove the bracelet from the small opening in the glass cabinet and when star witness Padilla insisted that the bracelet had been put in the left hand pocket of his jacket, Moore, laughed out loud as he indicated to the judge that there was no such pocket in the same clothing which he was wearing at the hearing. Moore was invited to cross-examine the witnesses and concentrated on the clearly nervous, chain-smoking, young woman, Senorita Padilla who spoke fluent English, later recalling: 'I knew she was jumpy and she had told so many conflicting stories that I couldn't understand anybody taking her seriously. I gave her the old Muhammad Ali stare for a few seconds and broke her story down'. On 29 May, the defendant was conditionally released on bail by the judge who pronounced that there was not 'enough evidence at the moment to justify the charge of theft'. Dr Andrew Stephens, chairman of the FA, who had stayed in Bogota throughout the four-day drama paid this tribute to the England captain: 'I never knew Bobby very well before. But he has opened my eyes through all this sorry business. He has been splendid from first to last – calm, undismayed and always with a sense of humour. I am proud of him'. An example of the prisoner's humour emerged with a story of how one of his personal guards asked him for a souvenir, 'Certainly', answered the soccer player, holding out his wrists as if to be handcuffed, 'If you give me a pair of bracelets…'.

The relieved player was allowed to re-join the team and received a hero's welcome in Mexico at the England camp in Guadalajara where he arrived with just five days to prepare before the team were due to play their opening match of their World Cup final campaign against Romania. The England team was considered to be even stronger than the one that had won the World Cup with six veteran campaigners: Bobby Moore, Gordon Banks, Alan Ball, Bobby Charlton, Martin Peters and Geoff Hurst joined by first choice full backs Keith Newton and Terry Cooper; centre-back Brian Labone; midfielder Alan Mullery and forward Francis Lee. Progressing to the quarter-finals, despite losing unluckily by the only goal of the game in the group stages to eventual winners Brazil, England faced their old foes West Germany. A popular conspiracy theory, of a South American plot to unsettle the England squad, flourished following the arrest of Bobby Moore and gained fresh impetuous when goalkeeper Gordon Banks was stricken with a mysterious case of food poisoning after eating a 'dodgy lasagne'. Deputy goalkeeper Peter Bonetti was drafted in as a late replacement and England built up a two-goal lead before disappointingly losing by the odd goal in five after their opponents had levelled the scores in the second half and taken the match into extra time. Against England, West Germany avenged their 1966 World Cup final defeat before losing the subsequent semi-final with Italy. The England v West Germany game was played in stifling heat at an altitude of 6000 feet, and *The Times* made the following comment about the display of the England captain: 'Bobby Moore, with Bogota now a distant memory, played a superb part in frustrating the German attack, who had scored more goals than any other country so far'.

Back in England, the two Bobby's reiterated their stories in a sworn statement requested by the Supreme Court in Bogota where three judges considered the preposterous charges against them. During this period, Bobby Moore faced another dramatic ordeal after a plot was uncovered to kidnap his wife Tina and hold her for a ransom of £10 000. Throughout August 1970, armed police mounted a 24 hour guard on the family home in Chigwell with detectives also accompanying Tina on shopping trips and keeping watch on the couple's two children as they played at the park. Faced with these difficult circumstances, Bobby Moore pulled out of a pre-season friendly for West Ham and explained to the press that a 'whispering campaign' had been on-going against him since his return home that had unfairly impacted on his family: 'All I want is some peace and quiet for my wife and children – they are not used to this upset and worry. I find that I am hardened to it after the Bogota affair with the bracelet'.

Despite Clara Padilla subsequently retracting her allegation claiming she was 'confused' and police reports that a female suspect had been spotted trying to sell the 'stolen' bracelet, the judicial process dragged on for five years without resolution with Moore continually facing the prospect of extradition to answer the trumped-up charges. The accusers became figures of hate in their own country and Danilo Rojas closed down his jewellery shop six months after the scandal broke. Clara Padilla was dismissed and temporarily sought refuge with family members in the USA. Colombian justice appeared to be a contradiction in terms with a decision on four out of five legal cases never determined. In November 1972, Bobby Moore was declared the victim of a plot by a Colombian court, when the former owner of Green Fire, Danilo Rojas, together with salesgirl, Clara Padilla and witness Alvaro Suarez were charged with extortion, blackmail and false testimony. However, the case was finally dropped without action three years later and, with no hope of being formally exonerated, Moore expressed his dismay: 'I wanted my name cleared... I was innocent and I wanted the world to know I was innocent. It made me sick to my stomach that some people still thought I had that damn bracelet'.

Football legend Bobby Moore amassed a then record of 108 appearances for England before his international career ended in 1973. England manager Sir Alf Ramsey once paid a glowing tribute to Bobby Moore: 'My captain, my leader, my right hand man. He was the spirit and heartbeat of the team. A cool, calculating footballer I could trust with my life. He was the supreme professional, the best I ever worked with. Without him England would never have won the World Cup'. After elimination from the 1970 World Cup in Mexico, England didn't even qualify for the final stages of the tournament until 1982 and, with a series of more failed bids and diminishing expectations of a team emerging to equal the feat of the 1966 World Cup team, a tribute to Bobby Moore, who died from cancer aged fifty-one in 1994, appeared posthumously in the Talk Talk Sports book of *100 Greatest British Sporting Legends*:

The Jules Rimet trophy glitters like the Holy Grail. And golden-haired captain Bobby Moore, beatific smile on his face, is held shoulder-high like a religious icon. As the decades pass, with decreasing hope of England ever being able to repeat their solitary World Cup win, those images of 1966 grow ever more ethereal and distant, like a vision of Heaven.

10
THE MYSTERY OF THE JULES RIMET TROPHY
1983

The World Cup is a very important way to measure the good player and the great ones. It is a test of a great player.

Pele (Fifa Player of the Twentieth Century)

The Holy Grail of soccer, the Jules Rimet trophy, was named after a French lawyer who served as president of the Federation of International Football Associations (Fifa) from 1926–1954. Designed by French sculptor Frances Abel Lafleur, the trophy depicted Nike, the Greek goddess of victory, arms upraised, holding an vessel, made of gold with an octagonal base of semi-precious stones valued at £30 000 when it was commissioned by Jules Rimet in 1930.

In 1966, the soccer world was stunned when the trophy was stolen in broad daylight and just as perplexed when, a week later, the gold figurine myster-

Jules Rimet (left) with the trophy named in his honour.

iously turned up abandoned on the pavement of a London street. When local resident David Corbett found his dog Pickles sniffing at a parcel in a hedge outside his home, he reached down to pick it up, untied the string and removed the paper packaging. As he unwrapped the object, he felt a thrill of excitement as he instantly recognised the significance of a list of names on the base that revealed the previous winners of the World Cup: 1930 Uruguay, 1934 Italy, 1938 Italy, 1950 Uruguay, 1954 West Germany, 1958 Brazil, 1962 Brazil.

At the outset of the Second World War, the Jules Rimet trophy was held by the 1938 winners Italy and placed in a Rome bank for safekeeping. Football's greatest prize was subsequently sought by Nazi treasure hunters who were thwarted by soccer official Ottorino Barassi. The Fifa vice-president smuggled the trophy out of the bank and risked his life by hiding it in a shoebox under his bed as enemy officers followed the scent and ransacked his home in a fruitless search. This story of wartime heroism to protect the World Cup made the appalling breach of security in London all the more embarrassing for the FA. When news of the national scandal broke prior to the 1966 World Cup finals in London, an incredulous Abrian Tebet of the Brazilian Sports Federation told the press in Rio Janeiro that such an outrage could never have happened in the country that had totally embraced the ethos of *jogo bonito* – 'the beautiful game' and commented: 'Even Brazilian thieves love football and would never have committed this sacrilege'. Those rash words would come back to haunt him after Brazil added to their World Cup triumphs of 1958 and 1962 with an overwhelming 4-1 final victory over Italy at Mexico City in 1970. 'Samba soccer' ruled the day as the ex-kings regained their crown in an exuberant exhibition of flair, skill and cobra-like striking to achieve a pinnacle of excellence never surpassed in the history of the game. Soccer writer Brian Glanville summarised the celebration which 'took on the dimensions almost of an allegory':

Pele played in his first World Cup final at the age of seventeen.

The Brazilian jubilation afterwards was as spectacular and memorable as anything one had seen on the field: a joyful, dancing invasion of fans milling around their victorious players, pulling off their bright yellow shirts and hoisting them, bare to the waist, onto their shoulders. In this exuberance, this unconfined delight, one seemed to see a reflection of the way Brazil had played; and played was, indeed, the word. For all their dedication, all their passion, they and their country had somehow managed to remain aware that football was, after all, a game; something to be enjoyed.

So the Jules Rimet Trophy, won by them for the third time, went permanently to Brazil, who had shown that enterprise, fantasy, attacking play were still compatible with success; provided you had the talent. There could be no comparison with England's brave but ultimately sterile victory of 1966, a victory which had led only to myths of 'athletic football', 'work rate', the elevation of the labourers above the artist.

The only danger to Brazil not receiving the Jules Rimet trophy during their fantastic final triumph was posed, not through any threat from the Italian team, but, from the hordes of their own delirious followers who swarmed across a moat surrounding the pitch at the Aztec Stadium. At the end of the game, souvenir hunters besieged the players who had their shirts ripped off and were subjected to physical danger as they were hoisted shoulder-high then carried on a perilous lap of honour by joyous fans. As writer Pat Collins observed in the annual *Charles Buchan's Soccer Gift Book*: 'The precaution of presenting Carlos Alberto with a replica of the World Cup, just in case, was seen to be just about the best move of the afternoon'. However, fears for the safety of the original Jules Rimet trophy were only temporarily averted and Brazil was plunged into a virtual state of national mourning when the cup was stolen thirteen years later. Having become the first country to win three finals, the country was awarded the Jules Rimet trophy outright and it was proudly displayed at the headquarters of the Confederation of Brazilian Football in Rio de Janeiro. The trophy was kept in a bullet-proof glass case on the third floor of the building, until, late in the evening on 20 December 1983, two hooded thieves broke into the premises, then, overpowered, tied-up, blindfolded and gagged the night-watchman. The robbers then patiently spent three hours hacking away the wooden surround of the display case before removing the World Cup and other trophies. Brazilian soccer president Giulite Coutinho immediately offered a substantial reward on behalf of the insurers, the Rio de Janeiro state bank, and made it perfectly clear that he was 'open to negotiations' with the thieves in regard to ransom. Standing by the empty display cabinet he waxed lyrical about the missing trophy: 'Its true value is spiritual. This was part of the nation's historic treasury. We're not talking about the material value of the cup. The important thing is what it represents because of the international prestige Brazil gained when it won it'. Despite the appeal for its safe return, the thieves evidently had no feeling of patriotism as the Jules Rimet trophy was lost forever. An exact replica of the trophy was commissioned from a mould made by the Germans when they won the World Cup in 1954. The duplicate of what was described by Giulite Coutinho as the 'symbol of the nation's primary sport' was displayed on a triumphant nationwide tour before being officially handed over to the Confederation of Brazilian Football at a ceremony held before a friendly international played between Brazil and England. The match was played at the Maracana Stadium, in the shadow of Sugar Loaf Mountain, Rio Janeiro, on 10 June 1984. The irony of the presentation taking place at a match between the two nations, who shared the off-field disgrace of losing the Jules Rimet trophy to criminals, was compounded when England winger John Barnes weaved his way from the halfway line beating five defenders to score a dazzling wonder goal. It was a brilliant moment, worthy of the English supporters' oft-repeated terrace chant of 'It's just like watching Brazil'. With debutante striker Mark Hateley also getting on the score-sheet in a famous 2-0 victory, England inflicted the first defeat suffered on home soil by Brazil since 1957. The result of the game, played in Rio with its famous landmark statue of Christ the Redeemer, was lauded by an ecstatic British press as the 'Maracana Miracle'. Furthermore, the soccer correspondent of the *Times* compared the feat to that of an English mountaineering nanny: 'The triumph was momentous, as historically significant as the day in 1817 when Henrietta Carstairs climbed Sugar Loaf Mountain for the first time and planted on top of it a Union Jack'. Nearly thirty years after the match, John Barnes recalled the highlight of his international career in an interview with the *Daily Mirror*: 'It was an iconic goal because it was in the Maracana, where Pele played. That mystique and magic of playing against Brazil in the Maracana will always be special'.

The fate of the original Jules Rimet trophy in Brazil remained a mystery. The police investigation concluded that, with several covert foundries around the city, it had in all probability, been melted down for gold bullion.

Pele scores in Brazil's 5-2 win over Sweden in the final of the 1958 World Cup.

An inquiry pursued the theory that the robbery was an 'inside job' and the night watchman's inconsistent version of events was viewed with suspicion. The day after the theft, two men, who had previously worked at the offices as janitors, were arrested, but with a lack of evidence, the suspects were released without charge. In December 1989, one of those arrested men, Antonio Carlos Aranha, was found dead having been shot seven times and his killer was never brought to justice.

Surprisingly the feelings of anger and national shame that greeted the theft of the Jules Rimet trophy were not shared by Brazilian soccer idol Pele who had done so much to win the cup with his brilliant performances as a member of the 1958, 1962 and 1970 World Cup squads. Pele the 'Black Pearl' formerly known as Edson Arantes do Nascimento, voted sports specialists' Fifa Player of the Century ahead of Johan Cruyff (Netherlands), Franz Beckenbauer (Germany), Alfred Di Stefano (Argentina), Diego Maradona (Argentina) and Ferenc Puskas (Hungary & Spain), graciously showed some sympathy for the light-fingered perpetrators, blaming the robbery on Brazil's economic plight: 'It is not the fault of the thieves, but of the authorities, because the people are desperate, without money and without food'. Having emerged to world prominence from an impoverished background himself, Pele recognised that he had been blessed with a gift for the game which had brought him honours, riches, and hero-worship, summarised in a quote he made without a hint of arrogance: 'I was born for soccer, just as Beethoven was born for music'. Mario Americo, Brazil's masseur at the 1970 World Cup finals in Mexico observed: 'Pele was so focused on winning the trophy. It was like it was his destiny. He was like a child waiting for Santa Claus'. Unfortunately, not every soccer-loving youngster who kicks a ball can make a living from the game, let alone be a genius like Pele, but, the joy of football provides an escape from the country's widespread poverty – an issue summed up in a poem by Oriosvaldo Almeida: it was inspired by watching children playing out the rather less than beautiful game of life on the crime-ridden streets of Brazil:

Children on a Spree

The children kick
Plastic bottles
As though they were the best
Footballs in the world.

The children kick mouldy cucumbers,
Screwed up balls of paper
And oranges,
As though they were the best
Footballs in the world.

The children make a goal
As though it was the very best
And most beautiful in the world.

They dribble through life,
Bruise their feet
Run and attack
No-one holds them back.

Life for them
Appears dynamic;
Their life is a dream
The dream to be one of life's
goal-scorer's.
The daily dream
To be a survivor.

Pele with his son Edinho who was sentenced to 33 years imprisonment in 2014

Poverty became a contentious issue leading to violent crowd demonstrations over the astronomical amount of public money lavished on football facilities when Brazil hosted the World Cup finals in 2014. Pele added his voice to the criticism: 'It's clear that politically speaking, the money spent to build the stadiums was a lot, and in some cases was more than it should have been. Some of this money could have been invested in schools, hospitals … Brazil needs it'. Due to Pele's earning power, his seven children had not experienced deprivation and social inequality in the football-mad nation, although, this did not prevent one of his sons, Edinho, from falling foul of the law. Having followed his father into professional football as a goalkeeper and then a coach, Edinho developed a substance abuse problem and was arrested at the age of forty-three on multiple charges of money laundering for a cartel that shipped cocaine into Rio de Janeiro. At his trial, held just days before the start of the World Cup finals in 2014, the court heard that Edinho had used his illustrious family name to provide an air of legitimacy to businesses that handled the money made from drug trafficking. The defendant was sentenced to thirty-three years imprisonment, then instigated a legal challenge against the verdict with the influential support of his father who declared from the outset: 'God willing, justice will be done. There is not a shred of evidence against my son'.

11
EXTRA TIME: SOCCER CRIME IN THE MODERN ERA
1992 - 2015

I'm more worried about being a good person than being the best footballer in the world. ... When I retire, I want to be remembered for being a decent guy.

Lionel Messi (Thrice World Soccer Player of the Year who was charged with tax fraud in 2015)

The domestic soccer scandals recalled in the preceding chapters occurred during the period in the far off days before the creation of the modern day Premier League, The Championship, League 1 and League 2 – a system that replaced a simple numerical system of First, Second, Third and Fourth divisions – in 1992. Whereas old-time miscreants like Billy Meredith and Sandy Turnbull may be viewed with the passing of time as merely 'characters' or 'loveable rogues', perhaps the most distressing historic cases are those involving famous footballers, Sandy Young, Tony Kay and Peter Swan, who fell from grace and served terms of imprisonment - a defining moment in their lives - although the stigma of a court appearance rarely has a damaging effect on the future of the modern player. In 2010, Manchester City's controversial Argentinian international Carlos Teves candidly admitted that if it were not for football, 'I would be in prison', however, in recent years, several top footballers have suffered this fate whilst actually engaged in the profession then, in many cases, unashamedly resumed their soccer careers despite being labelled as role models who have brought the game into disrepute.

Mickey Thomas became the first high-profile criminal casualty of the modern era. Capped fifty-one times by Wales, he had enjoyed a long career at the top level with several clubs including Manchester United, Everton and Chelsea before winding down his career at Wrexham. In 1992, at the age of thirty-seven, he rolled back the years and scored a spectacular free-kick in a shock FA Cup win over Arsenal. A year later he slipped from hero to zero when jailed for eighteen months on charges of laundering counterfeit banknotes via the unwitting trainees at Wrexham. Upon his release from prison, he cashed in on his notoriety on the after dinner circuit. The 'Welsh Tenner', who had never earned more than a basic salary of £25 000 a year from the game, regaled audiences with a joke about the escalating wages now on offer to footballers in the newly created money-spinning Premier League: 'Roy Keane is on fifty grand a week. So was I until the police found my printing machine'.

Duncan Ferguson, an aggressive 'hard-man' known affectionately to the fans as 'Dunc and Disorderly' racked up four convictions for assault resulting from an altercation with a fisherman in a pub, head-butting a policeman, kicking and punching a supporter on crutches and a three-month prison sentence for the infamous on-field 'Scottish kiss' inflicted on Raith Rovers' John McStay whilst playing for Rangers in 1994. By the time the case went to court the Scotland international striker had moved across the border to ply his trade with Everton and endeared himself to the supporters by appearing in the club's FA Cup winning side in 1995. In 2009, 'Big Dunc' and the disgraced 1960s England international Tony Kay were proudly inducted into the Everton 'Hall of Fame'.

Joey Barton, described on his personal website as a 'footballer', 'philosophy student', 'future coach' and 'fluent French speaker', also

"Would you mind answering a few questions about that last challenge?"

boasts that he 'won over' Oxford University students with an 'inspirational' talk and appeared as a guest on the prestigious BBC political television programme *Question Time*. Since his emergence as a pseudo-intellectual, he has helped Newcastle United (2010) and Queens Park Rangers (2014) to gain promotion to the Premier League having previously been sentenced to a total of ten months imprisonment during his career. In July 2008, the England 'one cap wonder' was given a four-month sentence after admitting assault occasioning actual bodily harm on teammate Ousmane Dabo during a training ground dust-up at Newcastle. Two months earlier, he had been sentenced to six months after being found guilty of assault and affray during an incident described by the trial judge as a 'violent and cowardly act'. The footballer was captured on CCTV punching one man twenty times then attacked a teenager during a boozy night out in Liverpool.

Lee Hughes received a six year prison sentence for causing death by dangerous driving after pleading not guilty to killing a middle-aged father of four in 2003. The West Bromwich Albion player had been driving in his £100 000 Mercedes and fled from the scene before giving himself up to the police thirty-six hours later. Appropriately, the jury took ninety minutes to reach their decision and the striker served three years before resuming his career with Oldham Athletic. On a similar charge, the most severe prison sentence imposed on a professional footballer in England was passed on Plymouth Argyle goalkeeper Luke McCormick who was jailed for seven years and four months after admitting killing two young brothers while driving dangerously at twice the legal alcohol limit in 2008. The crown court heard how McCormick was 'driving like an idiot' at around 90mph on a motorway as he returned from a wedding in his Range Rover. The former England youth international's lawyer desperately tried to elicit sympathy for his client by telling the jury that the goalkeeper had been upset and distracted at the time due to a malicious rumour concerning his fiancée and added: 'He was a professional footballer with a potentially glittering future. That was lost, and indeed lost forever'. However, that point proved not to be the case, for, after serving half of his sentence, McCormick was released on parole and, following a spell with Oxford United picked up his career with Plymouth Argyle where he was controversially made club captain in 2014.

Delroy Facey, formerly a striker with ten clubs including Premier League teams Bolton Wanderers, West Bromwich Albion and Hull City, was jailed for two-and-a-half years in April 2015 for bribing non-league players to fix the results of matches. There may have been misplaced sympathy for professional footballers of the past who erred while earning low pay from a short playing career. However, the theory that they may have been tempted into illegal match-fixing and betting activities to supplement their income surely does not apply to 'Del-Boy' Facey whose motives for a similar crime appear to financial greed. Rejecting the defendant's claim that he was an innocent party who thought two corrupt businessmen who offered him up to £15 000 for his part in the plot were 'class clowns' whom he decided to 'humour', the trial judge condemned Facey's actions for abusing his position as a role model to football followers: 'It's about the fans of the teams involved, the families who follow the fortunes of their teams with passion, loyalty and devotion. You have betrayed all that trust, all that confidence and it's like a cancer at the heart of football'.

Marlon King racked up twelve clubs and fifteen convictions during a playing career that included spells with Premiership clubs Watford, Hull City, Middlesboro and Wigan Athletic. The serial offender regularly appeared before the courts on a host of charges involving a wounding

"Well, you're my agent, who's offering the best deal – United or City?"

incident while playing amateur football, criminal damage, attempting to obtain property by deception, drink-driving and various other car motoring offences including handling a stolen car for which he was jailed in 2002. The Jamaican international striker later served eighteen months for sexual assault after groping a woman and breaking her nose in 2009. Then, in May 2014, he was jailed for a third time, receiving eighteen months for dangerous driving after deliberately braking and causing a pile-up while eating an ice-cream at the wheel of his Porsche. The court was doubtless relieved to hear, that following his retirement from football, the defendant was planning a new life with his wife and family in Zambia.

Ched Evans was singularly unfortunate when football turned his back on him following his release from prison in 2014. The Sheffield United striker had served half of a five year sentence for raping a drunken girl in a hotel room while two of his chums filmed the event. Unrepentant for his behaviour, apart from the pain he'd caused to his supportive partner on whom he'd cheated, the jobless striker launched an appeal against his conviction on the grounds that sexual intercourse had been consensual with the inebriated victim – who had subsequently been forced to go into hiding and change her identity after receiving online threats from 'trolls'. The case stimulated a debate about the right of an individual to rehabilitation when angry protests from supporters and sponsors prevented the Welsh international from signing for a string of clubs. Sheffield United, Oldham Athletic and Hartlepool United all dropped their interest in the wake of a backlash from supporters who far outnumbered the outcast's sick fans who made a series of vile chants of which the following is a relatively mild example:

There's only one Chad Evans,
One Chad Evans,
He booked a hotel,
Ended up in a cell,
Walking in a Evans Wonderland.

John Terry, once condemned in a tabloid newspaper as 'a serial brawler, drinker and womaniser', led Chelsea to the championship of the Premier League in 2014-15. During the season the club was shamed by a small number of their supporters visiting France to watch their team play a European Champions League match against Paris St Germain. A group of loutish thugs prevented a black passenger from boarding a train on the Paris Metro while chanting, 'We're racist, we're racist and that's the way we like it' while one of the culprits tweeted, 'Our captain is a racist, a racist, a racist and that is why we love him, we love him, we love him'. This was a reference to their hero's arrest following alleged comments made to opponent Anton Ferdinand during a league match against QPR in 2011. John Terry was tried and acquitted on a charge of racial abuse, but as ex-footballer Garth Crooks, of anti-racism in football campaign 'Kick it Out', commented in a television interview, that it was 'only half-time' for the accused who was hauled before an FA panel in October 2012. In stark contrast to the trial jury, the panel found the former England captain's defence to the charges 'improbable, implausible and contrived' and imposed a four match ban and a fine of £220 000.

Jermain Pennant was signed on a four-year deal by Liverpool in 2006. A year earlier, the winger had the distinction of becoming the first Premiership player to wear an electronic tag when appearing for his previous club Birmingham City. The England Under-21 player had been paroled from prison after serving thirty days of a three month sentence. Driving whilst drunk and disqualified, he was arrested after crashing his car into a lamp-post. Pennant's team captain, Liverpool icon Steven Gerrard, was acquitted of affray in a Southport bar in 2009. The defendant's high-powered legal team convinced the jury that the accused had acted in 'self-defence' when allegedly punching a DJ three times in the face because he 'thought' the victim was about to strike him. The brawl began after the drunken Gerrard and a group of six friends (who all admitted charges of affray or threatening behaviour) complained about the type of music being played. Leaving court without a stain on his character, Gerrard was greeted by fans with wild applause and shouts of

"Cheer up! You'll soon be back in training when your electronic tag is fitted".

'Rocky'. Justice served and his reputation intact the player took his tally of England appearances to 114 and captained the national team at the World Cup finals in 2010 and 2014. The skipper's armband then passed seamlessly to another 'ton-up' international, Wayne Rooney, whose reported extra-marital dalliances, among other indiscretions, provided an ideal character reference to lead England's qualification campaign for the World Cup finals in 2018.

"Better not argue with this ref".

The sleazier side of the nation's favourite sport continues to provide a steady stream of morally bankrupt soccer millionaires believing they are above the law and heading for the courts, though hopefully, supporters, players and officials will never experience a similar scene to that witnessed in America when Michigan League referee John Bieniewicz was killed by a single punch thrown by footballer Bassel Saad. The weekend player objected to a second yellow card that was about to get him sent off the field of play. As the defendant was sentenced in March 2015 to serve a term of imprisonment from 8-15 years for involuntary manslaughter and ordered to pay restitution of nearly $10 000 for the victim's funeral, John Bieniewicz's widow symbolically held up the red card that her late husband was tragically prevented from showing to his killer. Judge Thomas Cameron told the accused: 'For better or worse, you've come to personify all that's wrong with many people's belief about the escalation of violence in sports'.

The view of Judge Cameron echoes the critical observations of sixteenth century social commentator Philip Stubbes – set out before the advent of

An early derby played on the streets of London.

organised soccer and the adoption of the laws of the so-called 'beautiful game' – in his derogatory pamphlet on 'abuses' in England:

Football playing… may rather be called a friendly kind of fight than a play or recreation, a bloody and murderous practice than a fellowy sport or pastime… And hereof groweth envy, malice, rancour, hatred, displeasure, enmity and… sometimes fighting, brawling, contortion, quarrel-picking, murder, homicide and great effusion of blood.

117

BIBLIOGRAPHY AND SOURCES

THE GREAT FIFA WORLD CUP ROBBERY
Journals and Periodicals
Daily Mail, Daily Telegraph, Guardian, Metro News, Sunday Times, The Times.
Website sources
BBC News:
Fifa: www.fifa.com

THE GREAT WORLD CUP ROBBERY
Charles Buchan's Soccer Gift Book 1966-67, London, Longacre Press, 1966
Hurst, Geoff. *World Cup*. London, Headline Publishing, 2006
The Football Association World Cup Report 1966, London. Football Association, 1966
Seddon, Peter. *Pickles the World Cup Dog and Other Unusual Football Obituaries*, London, Aurum Press, 2007
Journals and Periodicals
Charles Buchan's Football Monthly, Daily Mail, Daily Sketch, The Guardian, Sunday Express, The Times.

THE FA CUP BURGLARY
Butler, Bryon. *The Official Illustrated History of the FA Cup*, London, Headline Publishing, 1996
Tyler, Martin. *Cup Final Extra*, Hamlyn Publishing Group, 1981
Journals and Periodicals
Birmingham Daily Mail, Birmingham Daily Post, Claret and Blue, Penny Illustrated, Sunday Pictorial, Sunday Times, The Times, The Weekly Standard.
Website sources
Aston Villa FC: www.Avfc.co.uk
Birmingham Mail:

THE THEFT OF THE EUROPEAN CUP
Hill, Tim. *A Photographic History of English Football*, Bath, Parragon, 2005
Nawrat, Chris. Hutchings, Steve. *The Sunday Times Illustrated History of Football*, St Helens. The Book People, 1998
Journals and Periodicals
Birmingham Daily Mail, Birmingham Post, Daily Mail, Guardian, The Times.
Website sources
Aston Villa FC: www.Avfc.co.uk
Birmingham Mail:
BBC Magazine: newsbbc.co.uk

THE ILLEGAL PAYMENTS SCANDAL
Kelly, Stephen F. *Back Page United*, Harpenden. Aurora Publishing, 1990
Sanders, Richard. *Beastly Fury: The Strange Birth of British Football*, London, Bantam, 2010
Journals and Periodicals
Athletic News, Daily Express, Manchester Evening Chronicle, Manchester Evening News, The Times, Umpire.

LIFE BANS FOR MATCH-FIXING (1915)
Kelly, Stephen F. *Back Page Football*, Harpenden, Aurora Publishing, 1988
Kelly, Stephen F. *Back Page United*, Harpenden. Aurora Publishing, 1990
Journals and Periodicals
Athletic News, Daily Mirror, Kilmarnock Herald, Liverpool Post, Manchester Dispatch, Manchester Guardian, Sporting Chronicle, The Times.

PLAYERS' BETTING RING GAOLED
Kelly, Stephen F. *Back Page Soccer*, Harpenden. Aurora Publishing, 1988
Tibbals, Geoff. *Great Sporting Scandals*, London, Robson Books, 2001
Journals and Periodicals
Daily Express, Daily Mail, Daily Telegraph, Independent, People, The Times.

THE MURDER TRIAL OF AN FA CUP HERO
Butler, Bryon. *The Official Illustrated History of the FA Cup*, London, Headline Publishing, 1996
Seddon, Peter. *Pickles the World Cup Dog and Other Unusual Football Obituaries*, London, Aurum Press, 2007
Tyler, Martin. *Cup Final Extra*, London, Hamlyn Publishing, 1981
Journals and Periodicals
The Argus, Guardian, Liverpool Echo, Melbourne Argos, Ravine Herald (Australia), *The Scotsman, The Times.*
Website sources:
Everton FC: www.evertonfc.co.uk

THE MURDER OF A FOOTBALLER
Lester, Paul. *The Murder of Tommy Ball: An Aston Villa Tragedy*, Protean Publications, 1996
Pike, Philip. *Tommy Ball: A Football Fatality*, The Footballer, Volume 2, No 4, February/March 1990
Seddon, Peter. *Pickles the World Cup Dog and Other Unusual Football Obituaries*, London, Aurum Press, 2007
Journals and Periodicals
Birmingham Mail, Birmingham Gazette, Guardian, Sports Argus (Birmingham), The Times.

THE BOGOTA BRACELET INCIDENT

Charles Buchan's Soccer Annual 1966-67, London, Longacre Press, 1966

Charles Buchan's Soccer Annual 1970-71, London, IPC Specialist & Professional Press, 1970

Borrows, Tom (Ed): *100 Greatest British Sporting Legends*, London, Simon & Schuster, 2011

Powell, Jeff. *Bobby Moore: The Life and Times of a Sporting Hero*, 2006

Tibball, Geoff. *Great Sporting Scandals*, London, Robson Books, 2001

Journals and Periodicals

Charles Buchan's Football Monthly, Daily Telegraph, Guardian, The People, Sunday Times, The Times.

Website sources

West Ham United: www.whufc.com

THE MYSTERY OF THE JULES RIMET TROPHY

Atherton, Martin. *Theft of the Jules Rimet Trophy*, Maidenhead, Meyer & Meyer Sport, 2008

Glanville, Brian. *The Story of the World Cup*, London, Faber & Faber, 2010

Charles Buchan's Soccer Gift Book 1970-71, London, IPC Specialist & Professional Press, 1970

Journals and Periodicals

Daily Mail, Daily Mirror, Guardian, Independent, The Times.

Website sources

Catholic Aid for Overseas Development: www.cafod.org.uk

Fifa: www.fifa.com

Four Four Two: www.fourtwofour.com

SOCCER CRIME IN THE MODERN ERA

Seddon, Peter. *Pickles the World Cup Dog and Other Unusual Football Obituaries*, London, Aurum Press, 2007

Stubbes, Philip. *Anatomy of Abuses in England*, London, 1583

Journals and Periodicals

Daily Mail, Daily Mirror, Daily Telegraph, Guardian, Independent, Metro News, The Times.

Website sources

BBC News:

Internet Archive: www.archive.org

Joey Barton:

Premier League: www.premierleague.com

Wikipedia the Free Encyclopedia: www.wikipedia.org